I hope you enjoy my final family memoir, Auntie Imo. I'm glad that I ended this stage in my life with Mom.

Love,
Judy
9/21/17

The Years Come and Go

Calendars, Journals, and Conversations

JUDYTHE PEARSON PATBERG

(Mostly) Minnesota Editions

authorHOUSE®

AuthorHouse™
1663 Liberty Drive
Bloomington, IN 47403
www.authorhouse.com
Phone: 1 (800) 839-8640

© 2017 Judythe Pearson Patberg. All rights reserved.

Photo, front cover: Margaret Pearson
Photo, inside page: Zachary Patberg at the farm
Photo, Dedication page: Margaret and Roy Pearson at their 80th birthday party

Quotes from *Letters from the Farm* by Becca Stevens, 2015
Quote from *To Bless the Space Between Us: A Book of Blessings* by John O'Donohue, 2008
Quote from *A Year in Thoreau's Journal, 1851* reproduced from a greeting card

To order copies of the author's previous titles - *We Just Shoveled Two Feet of Partly Cloudy, From Peace Corps with Love, A Winter Sabbatical, Tribute: Three Lives Remembered,* and *Rushing to Sunset,* please contact (Mostly) Minnesota Editions; 261 Stags Run; Harbor Springs, MI, 49740; or email at: judythe.patberg@gmail.com

No part of this book may be reproduced, stored in a retrieval system, or transmitted by any means without the written permission of the author.

Published by AuthorHouse 08/30/2017

ISBN: 978-1-5462-0461-9 (sc)
ISBN: 978-1-5462-0459-6 (hc)
ISBN: 978-1-5462-0460-2 (e)

Library of Congress Control Number: 2017912622

Print information available on the last page.

Any people depicted in stock imagery provided by Thinkstock are models, and such images are being used for illustrative purposes only.
Certain stock imagery © Thinkstock.

This book is printed on acid-free paper.

Because of the dynamic nature of the Internet, any web addresses or links contained in this book may have changed since publication and may no longer be valid. The views expressed in this work are solely those of the author and do not necessarily reflect the views of the publisher, and the publisher hereby disclaims any responsibility for them.

All scriptures used are taken from KJV

The farm is as much a state of mind as a place. We can never be truly lost because we are always part of the farm no matter where we are.

And so the farm goes to seed. When seed gets buried in the ground, it breaks down its hard outer shell and new sprouts emerge. It's not that different for us. We are dust and to dust we shall return. We are so much like the fields we tend. All our journeys begin and end with God; the sign of life is how we make our song, even at our grave. That is the truth of farming and the truth of our faith. We must be down at the end of the journey and simply, somehow, go to seed.

Letters from the Farm

Dedication

This book is dedicated to my siblings: Joyce, Gayle, and Wayne in memory of our parents, Margaret M. Pearson and Roy E. Pearson.

She opens her mouth with wisdom. And on her tongue is the law of kindness. She watches over the ways of her household. Her children rise up and call her blessed; her husband also, and he praises her......Charm is deceitful and beauty is passing, but a woman who fears the Lord, she shall be praised.
Proverbs 31:26-30

Blessed is the man who remains steadfast under trial, for when he has stood the test he will receive the crown of life, which God has promised to those who love Him.
James 1:12

Contents

Dedication vii

Introduction xi

Chapter 1: 1983, 1988 – 1990 1
Chapter 2: 1991 15
Chapter 3: Hummingbirds 24
Chapter 4: 1992 - 1995 41
Chapter 5: 1996 – 1999 64
Chapter 6: 1996 89
Chapter 7: 2000 – 2002 112
Chapter 8: From the "Wild Flowers of
North America" journal 125
Chapter 9: 2003, 2004 168
Chapter 10: 2005, 2006 179
Chapter 11: 2007, 2008 210
Chapter 12: Faith Journeys 222
Chapter 13: 2009, 2010 235
Chapter 14: 2011, 2012 245
Chapter 15: The Buzzards of Life and
Margaret's Musings 280
Chapter 16: 2013 – 2015 288
Conclusion 307

Introduction

This book is about my mother and, to some extent, my father who was married to my mother for 70 years. My father died on September 21, 2015, and Mom followed him ten months later, on July 5, 2016. As is the case with many marriages, theirs was not idyllic – too many bumps in the road and personality clashes – but it endured through bad times and the many more good times. Love of God, their family, and the land formed and strengthened their bond over the years.

My goal in writing this book was to present and preserve the contents of Mom's journals and calendars in the most reader-friendly way I could. I felt it was important to do this for the same reason I wrote all my other books: to contribute to my family legacy so that future generations will have the privilege of knowing the wonderful people who came before them. In this book, they will have a glimpse of the everyday life of Margaret Pearson – the comings and goings of her children and grandchildren (and the cows!), her thoughts about living and God, and the kind of weather that existed in her time and place.

The book has 16 chapters, most of which contain Mom's journal entries that are presented in her own words and calendar information which I summarized because of the repetition. Each chapter contains her journal entries and/or calendar information for certain years, beginning with 1983 and ending with 2015. Some chapters are necessarily short because Mom produced sporadic journal entries and no calendars, or calendar information with no journal entries, while others are long because they include both journal entries and calendar information. In 1983, for example, she recorded two journal entries with no calendar, and then there is nothing until 1988 when she produced a calendar but no journal entries. In contrast, Mom wrote weekly journal entries for every month in 2001. The exceptions to the journal/calendar chapters are Chapters 3, 12, and 15 which are narratives, focusing on Mom's musings about life and the discussions she, Dad and I had about different spiritual matters.

Each chapter includes at least one Bible verse, either one that I know Mom liked or one that I think she would have liked. As everyone knows, Mom believed it was very important to read the Bible because the Bible is essential for knowing God and His will for our lives. She reminded me many times that, apart from God's word, mankind would never learn the message of salvation through our Lord Jesus Christ, a message that Mom believed was all-important for herself and her loved ones……and for the world.

Except for the narrative chapters, which are easy to read, I can understand how a reader would want to use this book as a kind of reference guide for consulting chapters which satisfy a curiosity about the weather patterns and family events for specific years in Mom's life. Regardless of the way you, the reader, use this book, I hope that *The Years Come and Go* will provide you with reading enjoyment and enrich your knowledge of Margaret and Roy Pearson, the heart and soul of the Pearson Family.

Judy Patberg
Sept. 21, 2017

Chapter 1

1983, 1988 – 1990

(1983 journal entries, 1988 calendar summary,
1989 journal entries and calendar summary,
1990 journal entries and calendar summary)

You did not choose me, but I chose you and appointed you that you should go and bear fruit and that your fruit should abide, so that whatever you ask the Father in my name, He may give it to you.
John 15:16

1983 Journal Entries

May 10

I hate the idea of Mom not being "next door." This is a new experience for me – I've always had her at hand.

Today I've offered many special prayers for Jon J. and the Shirley family – what great sorrow is theirs!

It's good to have Gayle and the children home to pop in at any time. God is so good – oh, that we might praise Him more and magnify His name.

<u>Note</u>: Grandma Rosie had moved from the farm to North Star Apartments in Roseau. She was only 81 years old and had raised all of her children on the farm and lived there, even after Grandpa died in 1974. Even though she was in relatively good health, some of her children thought that she should not live alone. Mom was not one of those who believed that Grandma needed to move, and she was very sad when it happened.

June 5

The crops don't look too bad despite the heavy rain. In fact, some look nice. Roy has been so concerned about not being able to pay expenses and interest this fall.

Wayne started working for a construction crew this month. It's lonely not having him pop in and out during the day. The "little ones" are such a joy and really keep the old tepee hopping. Pam and Wayne and Gayle and Bill work pretty steadily. What fun when Joyce, Rod, Shawn and Sharon come out, and now another seems to be added to the crew (Jerry). I am so blessed with so many loved ones around me.

Last Sunday the airplane came to spray the barley. What a riot! So much excitement for doing so little?

Today I spanked Katie and Tony. I felt so downhearted, but they were real friends the rest of the day. I pray that they understand why and not think of me as an ogre – I love them so much.

Mom left for Uncle Christ's in Bottineau – she'll be gone a couple of weeks.

1988 Calendar Summary

Thirty-four calves were born from February 23rd to May 8th (exceptions: first calf was born the last of August, 1987 and the second one was born sometime in January). A calf was born to #91 on March 31st. On June 28th "a brand new "Si" (bull) joined the herd. Only one calf died this year.

During this year, Wayne sold cattle in January. The Farmer's Union dividend in January was $29.36 and January expenses totaled $106.25. Mom recorded expenses that included everything from antifreeze for the tractor ($22.23) to mineral blocks for the cattle ($7.00).

1989 Journal Entries

June 15

Today was such a pleasant day! Roy and I drove to Thief River and took Gayle, Tony, Joyce, Jena, Katie, Linsay and Rozie with us – all in one car! What a group of wonderful people – I love them all!

I pray for Wayne. He seemed so distressed this morning.

Tomorrow is the day – the girls and kids are biking to Roseau (It was a success!).

<u>Notes</u>: 1) Yes, the number of people in Mom and Dad's totaled nine! Of course, Jena was just a baby and Rozie only four years old, but, still, the conditions must have been crowded. 2) For a few years in a row, Joyce, Gayle and Pam, and whatever kids had the inclination, either walked, rollerbladed, or biked to Roseau, a mere 21 miles away. It took them most of the day to make the trip, and someone would pick them up in town to return home.

November 1

God is so good! Little Hannah will be all right. The hard fractures will take time to heal but there are no internal injuries elsewhere. Pam's ankle will heal also. Praise the Lord!

Note: Mom was referring to an accident when Hannah was about three months old. Pam was carrying her and slipped on some ice on the stairs and fell. She and Hannah had to spend a night in the hospital for observation because Hannah sustained a skull fracture and the doctor had to keep an eye on brain activity. Pam must have hurt her ankle in the accident.

November 3

Opening deer hunting weekend! Bill flew into Thief River and Roy went to pick him up. I pray that the "boys" will have a good relationship in their Jakt Stuga – and have good luck in getting their deer too.

August Eklund died after fighting cancer for some months. His life was a real testimony of faith in Jesus Christ as his personal Savior. He surely must have stored up treasures in Heaven.

I've definitely made the decision to retire after this term. To make it stick, I'm destroying materials as I go along. I still don't know if that's the way to go, but I'll just have to trust the Lord to lead me.

Note: The "Jakt Stuga" is a Norwegian term meaning "the shack." It is the place where the men in our family stay while they hunt and spin yarns around the campfire after a day of hunting. Women are invited to the Jakt Stuga for after supper campfires and special occasions, such as kids' birthdays.

December 1

Judy and the boys arrived for their extended stay - it will be fun to have them here and get to know them. Can we all live together peacefully for four months, I wonder?

Note: Here Mom is talking about the sabbatical I was given by the University of Toledo in 1989-1990 when I took the boys to the farm for four months, so they could have the experience of attending a rural school and spending time with their cousins. My plan was to do some research in Mom's first and second grade classroom, a necessary requirement for my sabbatical request to be granted.

1989 Calendar Summary

Once again, Mom recorded the birth dates for all the 43 calves that were born during the period of March 4th to May 27th. The bulls got out with the cows on January 12th because of deep snow and again on January 21st. A cow aborted her calf the week of January 16th, and two little darlings died in April (one froze to death). May expenses included $496.82 for wheat seed, $10 for Bolus pills (calves),

$5 for fire repair, $17.40 for filters, $17.65 for a calf replacer, and $5.08 for a chain.

1990 Journal Entries

February 1

All fears have been put aside – we are having a great time. Wayne fixed up a little office and living quarters for Judy and the boys in his basement. That alleviated so much congestion in this little house. I'm really enjoying the boys and truly loving them. They are such good kids. Zachie has accepted the fact that he has a short fuse and is doing something about it – even laughing at himself!

Tony is making great strides at growing up and controlling his temper also. How I love them all!

It is such a mild winter – so much fun to be outdoors. The kids are really enjoying themselves with their cousins. We get to snocat without freezing.

Two weeks later: Everyone left for the annual Presidents' Day ski weekend at Boyne. That's cruelty to old people! I'm so used to having 12-15 people around that living alone is hard to handle.

Everyone returned safely – happy and tired. Thanks to God once again for His protective hand.

February 23

Jenny starts work at the Patch; Chris is already working at Farmer's Union. They want the extra money but a lot of freedom will be sacrificed. Chris wants to buy a four-wheeler and a helmet.

April 1

Judy and the boys left for home this weekend. I hope they enjoyed themselves here, but I know they were anxious to get home.

They had car trouble in Janesville (again!) – must be their nemesis. The transmission ceased to work so Bill had to drive from Toledo to pick them up and then return to Janesville for the van later.

<u>Note</u>: Mom's "again" refers to a car accident we had in Janesville in 1982, when Willie was four and Zach two. That time, we were also returning from the farm where we had enjoyed a wonderful summer vacation. It was a more serious accident, unlike this incident which only involved car trouble.

April 8

More snow now than all winter long – seven and a half inches fell last night.

Easter came and went. We had a good day. I called Judy and her family – her voice is still gone from the cow incident!

Note: While I was home those four months, Wayne, Mom, Dad and I arranged a schedule whereby one of us would check the pasture at various times during the night for calves that had recently been born. On one of those nights, I had the two o'clock run so I made my way into the middle of the pasture to see if any of those little darlings had been born. I shined my flashlight around the huddle and decided that all was well. On my way back to the fence, I heard a noise behind me and looked back to see a cow rapidly picking up her pace. It was when I thought I could feel her breath on my back that I knew I was in trouble. I ran to the electric fence and realized that I couldn't get under it fast enough, so I picked up a stick that was lying on the ground, and brandished it in front of the cow until she retreated. During this whole time, I was yelling for Mom and Dad, who eventually heard me and came to my rescue. I had laryngitis for several months after that event. By the way, I held no animosity toward the mama cow…….she was just doing her job: protecting her baby.

May

So far a nice month – but sunny days are interspersed with lots of cold and some snow!

The last little calf was born on May 3rd – a nice, big bull calf.

We had our teachers' banquet on May 4th – I surely enjoyed it! We honored Lloyd who retired last summer and Jeannette E. along with a couple of bus drivers.

Little Hannah has been very sick with an infection in both ears!

I suppose this was my last spring program. This retirement decision is the hardest I've had to make. I've taught all my life and teaching has become a real part of me! But then, I'm resilient and can make a switch even at 64.

We had a very hard frost – down to 20 degrees.

Our trip to the Tetons was great. I never thought I would get to see so much natural beauty – breathtaking at times! Pam and Hannah and Sharon and Jena stayed home – we missed them very much and they were glad to see us when we got back. All that distance travelling and not one single mishap with either car – oh, how I praise the Lord and thank Him for His goodness!

Fall

Very, very dry – I wish it would rain but that too is something that God must handle. The garden was good, despite the lack of rain. The potatoes and corn are excellent.

We transplanted some strawberries and raspberries closer to the well so they could be watered. I really hope they'll winter okay. I miss having berries to eat and care for.

Pam didn't lose her job – instead she got full-time work doing what she enjoys. Everyone is busy. Sometimes I wonder what I would do without them all around. How blessed we are!

Life is progressing well without going to school. I enjoy subbing and it keeps me in the thick of things. I have no trouble keeping busy on the farm, helping with all that needs to be done before winter comes.

The children are all growing and everyone is an individual. Shawn and Dale aren't married yet – Dale says you can't rush into these things. He's very nice and is fitting into the group very well. Sharon is going with Andy who seems very quiet, but he and Sharon obviously like each other. And little Jena – what a doll! We surely love her and thank God for her – smart as a whip and a real bombshell.

Besides going to school, Jenny and Chris are working part-time – keeps them out of mischief and gives them the extra spending money they like. Jenny takes school very seriously and is on the A honor roll, but Chris is more nonchalant – he does okay and that's good enough. He has grown quite a bit this year and is becoming a good-looking young man.

Tony is a fifth grader and I believe that he's taking the responsibility for doing the best he can – and really, that's good. He too is growing up. Katie is in the 6th grade – I can't believe that she'll be in junior high pretty soon. She's a very good student and has a lovely personality. I think I'm losing Beezy – her activities keep her so busy, but, thankfully, she still finds time to stay with Grandpa and Grandma. Rozie is so cute and still likes to do things with Grandpa and me. Little Hannah is growing – not so much in stature, but in development. She walked very early and became independent very quickly – what a little imp!

Judy keeps us posted on Willie, Zach and Jon. I still get very lonesome for them and love them a lot.

The Christmas season is fast approaching. But the weather is not cooperating – very warm and no snow, like mid-October. Is this just a weather prank or is it part of the global warming they're talking about? Roy has talked about global warming for a long time. It frightens me!

Mom is so good. She went with us to the cookie exchange at Joyce's on Sunday – I think she enjoyed the company and baking.

Norma's little Derek died in November. They all grieve for him but God knows what is best. He didn't have a chance here and just think of how happy he is with Jesus. It must be especially hard for the family this time of the year.

Christmas

What a beautiful time of year! We got our snowfall earlier so it is very white and peaceful looking. But, as usual, the temperature slipped incredibly low – 30 degrees below and a little lower.

The children are such a blessing – they make every day worth living! Judy and her family could not be here this year but she makes certain that they are with us in love and in spirit. Gayle arranged for Santa to appear (isn't that just like her!) and the children's eyes almost popped out of their heads. Grandma Rosie was out and that always makes Christmas dearer. She's 86 but she's very active – I love her dearly. We have begun to go to Pam and Wayne's for gift opening – that was a brilliant move as they have so much more room. Christmas is Christ's birthday and we want more than anything else for Him to be present with us. How sad it would be if He didn't love us so much!

December 25: Wayne and Pam and girls and Sandy and her two girls left today for Arizona and New Mexico to visit Pam's brothers, Steve and Dave. They are stopping at Phyllis' along the way. It's a long journey and they will be gone for two weeks. Rozie was very "unsettled" about being gone so long and I'll be happy when they're home again. God, give them traveling mercies.

1990 March, April, May, and June Calendar Summary

Twenty-five calves were born in March, 14 in April (April 9th and April 30th in the snow) and two in May for a total of 41 calves. In June, there was a separation of the cows; some were herded into the draw and others went south.

1991

(1991 journal entries and March-October calendar summary)

Rejoice always, pray without ceasing; in everything give thanks; for this is God's will for you in Christ Jesus!
I Thessalonians 5:16

1991 Journal Entries

January 3

Gayle and Bill and family came back – they had a good trip.

January 9

Wayne and Pam and family also came home from Arizona where they had a good time. Now things will get back to normal. Sure was quiet around here. I'm glad that Joyce, Jena and the Warroad people were still around – it's always great having them close by.

January 15

Today's the day: Will we go to war? What a tremendous burden for us! Wayne shipped 30 head of cattle with Dwayne. I got to sub three days for Sara who miscarried – so sad.

<u>Note</u>: The war Mom mentions is, of course, Operation Desert Storm waged by coalition forces from 34 nations led by the United States against Iraq which had invaded Kuwait.

February 2

This morning I heard an unusual bird sing – very pretty. It's so mild.

I went to town early and stayed all day. I saw Tony play a hockey game, visited with Gayle, and went to see Grandma; Don and Gerry were there. In the evening, I watched Chris' team play, but they were so rough and tumble that I'm glad Chris didn't play much. Chris and I came home about 7:30, and we noticed that most of the fields were bare – must have really melted today.

Sunday – another unusually mild day; more snow melted. We all went on a picnic in the evening at Bemis Hill. The children had a great time.

The cows are taking advantage of the winter thaw — they're out grazing in the pasture and that's something for the beginning of February!

I'm going to sub for Sara on Thursday and Friday – great!

Note: This was early to have a picnic, even for the Pearsons who were noted for being the first to set out for Bemis Hill in the spring and the last to enjoy a picnic in the fall.

March 28

The baby calves finally began arriving – we now have about 16. They are so cute! That's one thing this dry weather is good for.

We are in Toledo – left a couple of days ago. The train was late coming into Grand Forks, so we had to wait at the depot until 2:45 a.m. Pam and Wayne and Hannah drove us down but didn't wait for the train – I'm sure it got late enough for them the way it was. We visited with Char and Allen until 11:00 or so and then Allen took us to the depot.

Grandma Rosie, Chris, Rozie and I had a good trip. The train ride went well – Mom didn't complain at all and tried to take everything in. Judy was happy to see us – she and Bill always make us feel so welcome. And the boys were happy to play with Chris and Rozie. I think that Mom was tired, though, by the time we got home.

April 12

By now, we have 38 little calves – the pasture is teeming with them.

Sharon Wensloff had her right breast removed on Monday. I was crushed to learn that she had cancer. Please, God, be the great physician and heal her body and spirit. She is such a wonderful young lady and she's my sister whom I love very much.

Four little pigs arrived this afternoon. The girls named three and left one for Tony. We're all excited but now there will be more work to do.

June 10

School is officially over and graduations were yesterday: Rozie graduated from kindergarten and Katie from sixth grade. Katie was first in the Malung-a-Thon and that really excited her. Beezy also did well – excellent jumper and runner.

We had Bible School last week – not a big enrollment but a good staff. Joyce, Sharon and Jena came out from Warroad and did the crafts section – Joyce does such a good job; she's so creative. Jenny helped also. She and Chris left for Wyoming on Friday, but they'll only be gone for 3-4 weeks this time. I'm glad they are not staying away all summer.

Father's Day

Our family left early Saturday morning for the Northwest Angle. We drove up and stayed overnight – the fishing was horrible but the day with everyone was great! Little Hannah just isn't ready for camping yet though.

We got four to five inches of rain last week – I think that will do us for a while.

Phyllis, Jessie and Kourtney are with Mom for about a month; they're staying at the house. It's so good to go home and find them there just as if nothing has changed – I hate change.

Judy, Bill and boys came home for a week – that just isn't enough time. Every time they come home, I get to know the boys a little better and I have such a special feeling for them. Each is so different – Willie is growing up fast and he was with Chris most of the time, doing "boy stuff." Zach, too, is a sweetheart, and Jon and Roz are good friends. How I love them all and miss them when they are gone. Judy is a good friend – she's easy to talk to.

July

In July, all the kids came over and painted the house a pretty gray – looks nice. Just before quitting time, about 8:00, Bill was painting the eaves and a wasp stung him right between the eyes. He had an immediate negative reaction. An ambulance was called, and Joyce took Bill from here at breakneck speed – she met the ambulance west of Salol. Bill was very close to death – what a hair-raising experience! I praise the Lord that Bill is still with us. We finished the painting at a later date.

Fred and Bev got their new trailer house – I like it very much.

Note: I just want to add that it was the quick action taken by Joyce that saved Bill's life. As the story goes, Bill actually wanted to take a shower before she took him to town, but Joyce wouldn't hear of it. She had just recently read an article about bee stings and how they can adversely affect people, given the right body chemistry.

September 5

School has started again: Katie is in the 7th grade in Roseau; Tony in the 6th grade in Malung with Mr. Klotz; Linsay in the 5th grade in Malung with Mrs. Czeh; and Rozie in the 1st grade in "Mannaska" with Mrs. Vatnsdal. Chris and Jenny are in the 11th grade this year – can you believe it?! I pray that each one will have a good year. How I love them all and pray that God will keep them in His care. He's the only one who can truly guide and lead them.

Judy has retired from her university position so that she can be a full-time wife and mother. She is really burned out and I think she'll enjoy caring full-time for her family. Willie is already a teenager – 8th grade and taking an active interest in the girls. Zach is in the 5th grade and Jonny in the 1st grade. They are all so active in sports as well as music, church and other things. Their lives are really on the move.

<u>Note</u>: I resigned, not retired, from The University of Toledo and taught English as a Second Language at Southview High School for four years. It was a welcomed change from the rigors of university teaching and publishing research. Then, in 1995, I was rehired and demoted: Having resigned as a full professor with tenure, I had to be hired back as an assistant professor! I had a rewarding second term and retired in 2010.

September 18

Snow – how about that for a record breaker! September is really a nice month – plenty of rain and the leaves are beautiful. We certainly had an abundance of tomatoes to care for and the potatoes are abundant as well – the first real fruit came during the last week.

I've started caring for Hannah full time. She is such a good little girl and so cute – we love her to pieces.

I guess school is going well for everyone. I am very glad for Tony – he likes Mr. Klotz and is actually quite a smart little guy. Chris and Jenny like 11th grade – Jenny and Tim broke up mutually. Katie is doing well in volleyball – she started band and plays the flute. Linsay leaves for a drug camp on Thursday and Friday. She was chosen to represent her class and when she returns she has to report to them what they should do and know (talk about being proud; she was bursting!).

We went to Duluth to watch the big ships – we saw two impressive ones. Stayed at Debbie and Steve's on Saturday night and came home on Sunday. Had a very nice time – the leaves were gorgeous.

December 31

The weather is very unseasonal. We have plenty of snow but the temperatures are so mild it makes snocatting fun because we don't have to worry about frostbite.

Christmas came and went so fast. It was a great time. Judy and Bill and their family were not home but the rest came for supper at 4:00. We had ribs and lutefisk – everyone ate too much. After supper, we all went over to Wayne and Pam's for gifts – such a good time. Maybe next year Judy and her family can be with us. Mom didn't come out – she went to Sharon's. Sharing isn't always easy. Gayle, Bill, Tony and I are going to Toledo on Friday after work.

1991 March – October Calendar Summary

As usual, Mom's calendar entries were taken up mostly with calving news: 18 calves in March with one death; 26 in April with one born in the snow and another with the misfortune of having a "mean mother"; and two born the last of May and the first of June........46 little darlings this year! It snowed and was very cold on April 14th and again on May 1st and 2nd. Si and Sam, the two bulls, received a lot of attention: Mom recorded what pastures they were currently residing in, who was being moved, and whether they were enjoying the company of their ladies or not. Then, Adolph arrived on June 26th, so there must have been three bulls cavorting in the pastures at one time. The cattle were, at various times, on Freddy's, in the draw, and up north. Two miscellaneous entries: a calf was born on August 11th; and three to four inches of snow fell on October 20th.

Chapter 3

Hummingbirds

Look at the birds of the air; they neither sow nor reap nor gather into barns, and yet your Heavenly Father feeds them. Are you not of more value than they?
Matthew 6:26

(One of my greatest joys of spending so much time on the farm with Mom and Dad during the last couple of years derived from the conversations we had about God, faith and life. Most of these conversations occurred while sitting on the porch in the late mornings and early evenings and in the living room where we would occupy our respective places: Mom in her rocking chair by the fire, Dad in his recliner and I in my chair; we formed a triangle of space often shared with Zeke and sometimes, Mack.)

There was a time in my life when I was faced with the difficult task of discerning my role as a leader in my church. I was going through the discernment process at church and was praying for an insight from God that would help me make my decision. One day I felt a pull – an inkling – toward saying yes, but it wasn't definite enough for me to feel secure in a decision to go ahead with this major commitment. I called Mom and asked her how we can know when an insight or an answer is from God and not something that comes from our own will for our lives. There was silence, and then she said that she thought the only way we can know an answer comes from God, and not from us, is by seeing how the situation turns out. If things work out, then it was the Holy Spirit helping us decide. If things don't work out, the insight or idea probably didn't come from God.

I was dubious. Is everything that works out for us a God thing? Should we assume that every insight for helping us make decisions, which turn out to be the right decisions, is from God and is a part of His will for our lives? Couldn't the insight have originated from our own will for our lives, as opposed to God's will?

Probably I was most troubled by the realization that I couldn't use this test………waiting to see if a decision works out was not going to help me make the decision in the first place.

In one of the books I read on spiritual matters some time ago, the author suggested that we can know if something is from God by asking the question: If we obey this insight, will it benefit others…….will it empower us to love others? When I introduced this thinking to Mom, she agreed that the criterion was probably a good one to use in a discernment situation, such as the one I was going through. She reminded me, though, that prayer is the key and I should keep praying.

Weeks later, Mom, Dad and I were sitting on the deck one late morning watching the gold finch, blue jays, sparrows and other bird species fight for room around the feeder. We began an on-going discussion about the Holy Spirit. I say "ongoing" because we never seemed to resolve the issue: Who has the Holy Spirit and who doesn't; where is the Holy Spirit present; and what does the Holy Spirit do? It's one of the few discussions that Dad participated in because he'd never felt the presence of the Holy Spirit in his life, and that fact weighed on his mind. Nothing Mom and I said could ever convince him that the Holy Spirit abides in us as a result of being a Christian and walking with Christ, and we don't need to feel its presence – feeling is not a necessary condition for the Holy Spirit to be present.

Mom, in her infinite patience, would explain over and over that Dad did have the Holy Spirit, that the Holy Spirit empowers us and enables us to be what God wants us to be. She told Dad that he wouldn't even be able to pray without the Holy Spirit's guidance or be able to understand the Bible during his devotions. She would emphasize that the Holy Spirit is God's gift to us. She would read to him from the Bible, from Romans: "And the Holy Spirit helps us in our distress. For we don't even know what we should pray for, nor how we should pray. And the Father who knows all hearts knows what the Spirit is saying, for the Spirit pleads for us believers in harmony with God's own will."

It didn't help matters that Dad's brother had a couple of emotional experiences where the presence of the Holy Spirit was overwhelmingly powerful in his life. Dad related those experiences many times, and each time he was filled with longing – he wanted that kind of experience desperately and prayed for it to happen. To my knowledge, it never did. We had our last discussion about the Holy Spirit a few days before Dad died. I pray that he derived comfort from believing that the Holy Spirit was with him.

There's a mystery about the Holy Spirit, and I admit the concept is difficult to understand. Sometimes I feel the Holy Spirit most of all in creation – in flowers, sunsets, and storms – when peace flows over me and I have a powerful feeling of safety in God. Mom also felt the presence of the Holy Spirit in the beauty of nature, including (especially?) pastoral scenes of cows contentedly chewing their cuds and little calves frolicking in the barnyard. She would sigh and say something about everything being okay.

Dad and I went on many walks together; even when his legs hurt him and he became short of breath, he would try to walk until he could no longer do it at all. I loved those walks, and I loved the fact that Mom would always be waiting for us when we returned to ask: "And how was your walk?" Henry David Thoreau (*A Year in Thoreau's Journal, 1851*) entered this in his journal: "Now I yearn for one of those old, meandering, dry, uninhabited roads, which lead away from towns – which lead us away from temptation......where you may forget in what country you are traveling; where your head is more in heaven than your feet are on earth. There I can walk and recover the lost child that I am without any ringing of a bell." This is the way I felt walking with Dad, sometimes talking but often in silence, which I found comforting. On some days, walking was how we muddled through, one day at a time.

During one of our conversations about God, Mom said she was aware of the possibility that if she had been born into a Muslim family, she would be practicing Islam today. She said that people of other religions, especially the Muslims, had been in her heart and on her mind a lot, and she knows that God loves them as much as He loves Christians. It was hard for her to reconcile this knowledge of a God who loves everyone, and doesn't want anyone to go to Hell, with her firm belief that Jesus is the only way to God and Heaven…….. she worried about the fate of all those who don't believe that. She listened respectfully to my suggestion that maybe we shouldn't put God in a box and should be open to the idea that He allows more than one pathway to Heaven. I think that suggestion worried her a little, however, because she said, "But, Judy, you believe that Jesus is the only way to Heaven, don't you?" I assured her that, as a Christian, I believed in Jesus as the way. The only explanation Mom could offer for the fate of those who don't believe in Jesus Christ is that God, in His mysterious ways, will take care of them, and we need to leave that which we don't understand to Him. She agreed with me when I suggested that wherever the virtues of compassion, mercy, forgiveness and love (the hallmarks of the Christian faith) are practiced, God could very well be present and celebrated.

Mom was intimate with Jesus and yet she was, at times, lonely and afraid. She usually had this kind of strong, calm persona, though, even in times of loneliness and fear. She drew comfort from the first part of Psalm 139: "Thou art the God of the early morning, the God of the late at nights, the God of the mountain peaks, and the God of the sea; but, my God, my soul has further horizons than the early morning, deeper darkness than the nights of earth, higher peaks than any mountain peaks, greater depths than any sea in nature. Thou who art the God of all these, be my God."

The hardest discussion we had on several occasions was about God's plan for our lives and the control He has over the decisions and choices we make. Does God have a unique life plan for each of us, and is our earthly task to discern and follow the path so that we can be happy and fulfilled? Mom believed that God knows what He wants for us and how we will turn out from the very beginning…..He has it all worked out for each of us. I asked her if she had a problem reconciling God's plan for us and His gift of free will: how could God give us the freedom to make our own choices and decisions if He already has a set plan for our lives that must be followed? (She interjected a little humor in one of our discussions when she said that God took a real risk when He gave us the freedom to choose.) She said that we make the choice to either reject or accept His plan, whatever it is. If we accept it, and stumble – which everyone does – God will help us find our way back. Maybe she's right: God has a plan for each of us – regardless of whether He reveals it – and it is up to us to figure out how to act in accordance with His plan. Mom believed that God had a plan for her life, and she fervently prayed that she was following His will. I told her that I felt the same way.

One thing I personally believe is that, while God has a plan for us, He doesn't want to control our lives; He wants us to be in control of our own lives, to make good decisions and choices that will improve the world in which we live. Mom believed that God was ultimately in control of everything......period.

Maybe the alternative to trying to discover God's plan for us is to try to follow Jesus – to lead moral lives, to take care of our fellow man and to put Him first in our lives. That's hard enough!

Sometimes at the end of the day, Mom, Dad and I would ask the questions: What did we learn today? What did we do to help someone? Why was I given this day? Mom's eyes were bad, and she tired easily, but she read every day – always her devotions, the newspaper, and her crossword puzzles - for as long as she could. She bemoaned the fact that, while she learned something every day, she forgot what she learned and could not share it with others. She would say, "What's the use of reading when I forget what I've read almost right away?" I would say, "It's the pure joy of reading, Mom, the pleasure you receive from reading an interesting fact or allowing yourself to become immersed in someone else's adventure, or enjoying the warm memories evoked by a descriptive passage – it's the joy of reading, just for the act itself."

Until he no longer had the attention span and the comprehension for reading anything longer than a short news story or his nightly devotions, Dad was a voracious reader. He would devour books given to him as Christmas gifts and borrowed from the library; he also read two daily newspapers which kept him informed of what was going on in the world. In his later years, however, his reading ability declined, and it was difficult to find material that could sustain his interest long enough for him to finish it. I missed that about him......eventually, there were very few topics we could pursue except for events that happened in his past.

When we asked ourselves what we did to help someone today, Mom would say, "All I can do is send money to charities, asking God to bless it, and pray." I reminded her that praying was the best thing she could do, and she shouldn't think of it as the least. Mom prayed all the time – conversations with God in the morning, throughout the day, and during the long night when she couldn't sleep. She praised God and thanked Him for her daily blessings. She prayed for everyone in the family (including Wayne's cows) and as the family grew, so did her prayer time. She also prayed unceasingly for those who needed physical healing or needed to be spared hardship, all the while acknowledging that it may not be God's will that her prayers be answered, at least not in the way and in the time frame she had in mind. We placed a lot of trust in my mother's prayers, believing that her faithfulness earned her a direct line to Heaven.

Can prayers shape the future? Mom believed they can. I had asked her why she thought we should pray when God knows the future and is already in control of everything. She said that many miracles have occurred because of prayers offered and cited instances in the Bible (e.g., Jonah) where God was affected by prayers so much He changed things. Mom believed strongly that God's decisions can be influenced by what we say and do……..so we should keep on praying until God grants our request or convinces us that our request is not His will for us. She said that God hears all our prayers but does not always give us what we pray for. He will answer in the affirmative if our request, in some way, increases our identification or recognition of Him. When our request is granted, we should know that our prayers contributed to the result: when it is not granted, however, it doesn't mean that our prayers weren't heard, but they were refused for our ultimate good and for the good of others. The relation between our prayer and something that happened is not mere coincidence……there's no empirical proof of this, just faith. Mom reminded me that we should pray even when we don't feel like it because God commands us to pray.

I told Mom one of the main reasons I pray is that I love communicating with God and experiencing His peace, which is unlike any other form of comfort I receive. She said that she also receives peace from praying. She believed that the most powerful prayer in the Bible is "Lord, help my unbelief." I think it's just plain "Help!"

I need to add that, in addition to praying, Mom performed intentional acts of kindness to people who needed some encouragement and assurance that God loved them. For example, she visited with her neighbor and brought her flowers to make her feel less lonely, and gave a homemade pie to another neighbor to show she cared about him (information from her calendar).......she failed to mention these little acts of kindness when we talked about what we do to help others.

I believe that if Mom had lived a different kind of life, one that had afforded her more opportunities to choose, she would have done mission work, probably in Appalachia. She was bothered by God's command that we are to feed the hungry and help those in trouble. And this brings me to the question we asked ourselves sometimes at the end of the day: Why was I given this day to live? To my knowledge, this question invited discussion but never really yielded an answer. Toward the end of her life, Mom would say, "I can't understand why God still wants me on the earth. I can't do anything anymore." Still, she believed that God had a purpose for her life. Dad would also wonder why he was still living at 88 or 89. And yet, both were grateful for another day of life......I believe that.

Mom was basically a happy person, and I believe her happiness stemmed from a spirit of gratitude. She was profoundly grateful for every day she was given and for everything she believed God had given her, mostly for the blessings of her children and grandchildren. At the end of each day – and in the middle of sleepless nights – she went through her day and thanked God for all the wonderful things that had happened to her and the people she loved. Sometimes she would softly sing hymns of praise throughout the night.

One day after Dad died, we were talking about how hard it is to be grateful when someone you love is going through difficult times or when the loss of a loved one creates a void in your life. Mom didn't allow me to complain or dwell on this difficulty long though; she reminded me that every day, with its sorrows as well as its joys, is a gift of life, and just the fact that we can walk and hear and see should make us grateful. I truly believe that Mom oriented herself to the world in a state of gratitude.

One of Mom's favorite verses in the Bible talks about how weeping may last through the night but joy comes with the morning. I know that there were many nights when Mom lay awake, unable to clear her mind of the day's burdens, waiting for the dawn to break forth with the sense of hope and joy that marks a new day. Night time fears moved aside for hope.

Mom, Dad, and I talked quite a lot about suffering...... mostly about how some people seem to be eternally blessed while others suffer immensely. Dad wondered why missionaries suffer when they are already sacrificing so much of themselves. He would remember Uncle Ed's girlfriend whom Ed loved very much. She chose a life on the mission field instead of Ed and then was killed in a car accident while home on furlough. Dad found it hard to believe that God would allow someone who was already serving Him to die like that. Mom brought up instances of violent suffering in the Bible, the worst being the killing of all first-born babies in the tenth plague. While being careful not to judge God, she did wonder why He couldn't have used another method to deliver His people from oppression. I told her it was that kind of violence, especially that which was condoned by God, that made me quit reading some of the Old Testament Bible stories to my children when they were little.

We even tackled the difficult question of how we make sense of suffering: why does a God of love and mercy allow suffering in this world? Mom posited that we suffer because we live in a fallen world, but what's more important than why we suffer is how we deal with suffering. We can either respond with bitterness and anger and a "why me" attitude, or we can respond with acceptance and hope, knowing that God can turn suffering around for our good, and we need to trust Him for things we can't understand. Suffering turns our thoughts to God and reveals what is in our hearts. She encouraged me to remember that, while God doesn't wish for us to suffer, He is with us in our suffering and, as Christians, we have hope in Jesus Christ. We talked about the two effects suffering can have on people: Suffering is something that can bring people close to God or it can turn people against God. If we think about how much we need God, our suffering should draw us closer to Him. And our faith should be strengthened. However, we both could understand why some people do not want anything to do with God after suffering from a terrible loss.

Does God feel our pain when we suffer? Mom was adamant in her belief that He feels our pain and never leaves us. He cannot eliminate the pain, however, without eliminating our freedom. We agreed that it is hard to understand the suffering of innocent children......our lack of understanding just makes us realize that, in the end, we have to trust in what we know about God and then surrender ourselves to Him.

While Mom worshipped with Dad at Bethel Mission Covenant Church all their married lives, she was baptized and confirmed as a Lutheran and attended Pine Grove Lutheran Church until she married Dad. The Covenant Church didn't perform infant baptisms, but Mom had all of us baptized as babies at Pine Grove. She was careful to stipulate that baptism doesn't save us, that only a personal commitment to Jesus Christ can do that, but I think she must have derived some comfort by having the mark of the cross placed upon our infant brows. We talked about the Lutheran promise given in baptism: We are made God's own and we inherit everything good that God wants to give us; that heritage is ours forever and it can never be changed. It's a powerful promise……that once God has made us His own, He will always recognize us as His own, and nothing can separate us from Christ. We have a God who will not let us go.

Toward the end of her life, Mom talked increasingly often about her desire to be reunited with her loved ones who had died. We agreed that living and dying are great mysteries and that the images of Heaven we read in the Scriptures are the best efforts of mere people to describe the infinite. We don't know what will come next in this life and we can't know Heaven. But we do know that our lives are in God's hands. While she wasn't sure what form the reunification with her loved ones would take, Mom hoped for the total renewal of all that they are – body, soul, and spirit. She used as the basis for her hope the fact that Jesus rose in body and not as pure spirit.

One of Mom's (and Dad's, I think) favorite hymns was "I Know Who Holds Tomorrow." I can still hear Mom singing, "Many things about tomorrow I don't seem to understand; but I know who holds tomorrow and I know who holds my hand." We agreed that, as we age, we seem to understand the world less and less and need to trust God more and more.

In her life, Mom witnessed many acts of God's love and grace. But she was continuously distressed by the hatred and evil depicted on television every day. She would say, "If only people would come to Jesus, their lives would be changed and there wouldn't be so much violence in the world." It was when she despaired the most, however, that she was greatly optimistic: She was sure that God's love and grace would ultimately prevail. Even with all her talk about God's love and grace, though, she didn't sugar-coat the need for us to be ready to meet Christ. She warned me many times (as she did my siblings, I'm sure) that we need to be ready to face Jesus at any and every turn. He could come again when we least expect Him, so we should keep praying and be ready.

On the morning that we were sitting on the deck watching the birds, a hummingbird missed the feeder and hit the deck rail with such force that it was clearly stunned. Mom held the tiny bird in her hand until it recovered. I noticed the gentleness and care with which she held the bird, not wanting to harm it. Gentleness was a quality of Mom's that I've always appreciated, always loved, because it pervaded all aspects of her life, including the way she handled people: very carefully so as to try not to do any harm. She was a very lovely person.

Chapter 4

1992 - 1995

(1992 journal entries and calendar summary, 1993 journal entry and calendar summary, 1994 journal entry and calendar summary, 1995 journal entries and calendar summary)

Jesus said, "Come to me, all you who are weary and carry heavy burdens, and I will give you rest. Take my yoke upon you. Let me teach you, because I am humble and gentle at heart, and you will find rest for your souls. For my yoke is easy to bear, and the burden I give you is light.
Matthew 11: 28-30

1992 Journal Entries

January

We spent New Year's at Judy's – had a very good trip to Toledo. Chris and Jenny flew in from Colorado. We had a great time together – saw "Father of the Bride" and then went to supper at a place where we had a delicious meal. Wonderful fellowship!

April

My, I've been slack in writing – wonder if I can catch up a bit. Our spring has been absolutely horrid – hot one day and cold and wet the next few. We had a total of 59 calves but two aborted and one died when it was a couple of days old. It was a stressful time. The barnyard was so wet that feeding was almost impossible. Every angle was used and day by day, they did get enough to eat.

The second year of my retirement came and went. I did a little substitute work but hope that next year will be better. I still miss the classroom.

June

Still cold and wet – frost on the first day of summer! But it was gorgeous the weekend of the Zorn reunion which was held at Malung, and it was a great success. Judy and Bill planned their vacation so that they could be a part of the celebration. Jon played his violin and Willie and Zach played "The Rose" on the piano and dedicated it to Grandma Rosie –both performances drew great applause.

Norma had surgery for cancer – most of her stomach and some lymph nodes were removed. What a shock!

July 18

We went to Baudette to see Norma and Brandon. Both are living at home, but they are very weak and thin. Time is needed in each case - praises to God for His unspeakable mercy to us.

Phyllis, Jessie and Kourtney spent a month at Grandma Rosie's house – I miss them greatly. Their presence at the house seemed to turn the clock back and we'd stop in there often – always activity, warmth and a good cup of coffee. No strawberry picking this year though – Phyllis was so disappointed. The cold season and lack of sunshine has made for a poor crop of this delicious berry.

The garden is late also. We have delicious onions because they like the cold – the peas have grown huge and are loaded with blossoms; hopefully, they will fill in time. Tomatoes seem to be hopeless but possibly will yield later on – Roy is very disgusted.

Judy called with some disturbing news – she is having trouble with her heart. More tests are being done tomorrow and we'll know more after she calls. My heart is distressed!

<u>Note</u>: After a number of tests, I was diagnosed with an abnormal heart rhythm that resulted in a crazy pattern on an EKG, which caused all kinds of concern. Finally, my doctor decided that this was a condition I was born with and, medically speaking, it is harmless unless the pattern changes. So, I use that EKG printout as baseline data and carry it with me in my wallet, in case of a medical emergency. The pattern has not changed over the years, and I continue to have no symptoms, so I think I'm going to be okay!

1992 Calendar Summary

In March and April, the prime calving months, the little darlings entered the world at a fast pace......every day there was a calving event, and Mom labeled each one. For example, on March 8th, a calf was born to "Little Heifer," and a couple days later the "Mean Angus" gave birth. On many days, there were multiple births: one day, a calf was born at 5:00 a.m., another at 10:00 a.m. and two at noon. Number 33 paired up with a black heifer, and their offspring was a red calf with a white face. Fifty-five calves were born in March and April, two in May, and two in June for a total of 59......it was a good year! The weather appeared to be normal for March but cold and snowy in April. It was a very wet spring. Two cows came down with foot rot, and Wayne had to give the calves pills and shots. According to the calendar notes, two calves died. Easter on April 19th was "nasty and rainy." There was a very hard frost on May 22nd, the same weekend that Si was with the white faces and Sam and Adolph with the Angus. On June 21st, Si bred his own red heifer. While Mom didn't mention a visit to Toledo on May 29th in her journal, she recorded that event on her calendar. The cattle were up north during the whole month of July and then in August went south on Freddie's, followed by a short sojourn in the little pasture by the barn, and ending up in the draw. August 21st brought hail and terribly heavy rains when there were 70 acres of hay down. The cattle were in alfalfa southwest of the house on September 4th, the same day that Wayne finished haying. He sold 20 head on November 2nd when three inches of snow fell. Mom noted on the calendar that the house was painted in 1991 and the grainery in 1992.

1993 Journal Entry

It's been a long time since I've written and a lot has happened. Norma died a few days before Christmas. I miss her so much. It still doesn't seem possible that she's dead. I was just getting to know her now again after all these years of raising our own families, etc. How I wish I had spent more time with her.

Irene had major surgery on her stomach – a huge benign tumor. She had her surgery in Bemidji and is recovering quickly and doing well.

Phyllis had colon cancer surgery last fall. That too was a trying time. She's very upbeat but I wonder at times how it really is. Both Trish and Lisa got married around Thanksgiving and Christmas. Many of us went to Oklahoma at that time. Phyllis is such a lovely person! I believe that God has touched her in a very special way and she is truly leaning on Him – isn't that great?! She's a good witness for the Lord to people around her. I just heard that both Lisa and Trish are having a baby so Grandma Phyllis will be plenty busy.

On December 23rd, I got up very early and felt that something was very wrong. A tremendous pain developed and spread across my chest – I was having a heart attack! The quick action of the kids plus a new heart medication confined the affected area of the heart so no bypass surgery was necessary. What an awful pain that was! I spent three days in ICU and four more days in the hospital. It's still hard to believe that it really happened. Everyone spent Christmas at the hospital and we postponed opening gifts until New Year's Eve. Needless to say, it was a totally different Christmas season! Judy and Bill and the boys were here. And was it ever cold – the water and sewer systems froze and they had an awful time. Here it is….Valentine's Day and nothing is working yet.

1993 Calendar Summary

It was a cold winter. Except for a warm spell during the last week in January and the first week in February (30 – 40 degrees), the two months were very cold (-30 to - 40 degrees). March and April produced 62 calves with a couple of stragglers entering the world during the "very cold month of May". Beautiful weather marked the first week in March, but it turned cold (15 – 20 degrees) the second week. Mom's calendar entries are very interesting to me because she not only records how many calves were born on a particular day, but also the time they were born and the conditions under which they entered this world. For example, a little calf was born at 2 a.m. on March 15th when it was 15 degrees below zero and, before he could be taken to a warmer place, he froze his tongue and had to be cared for in the house where he died two days later. Cow number 91 waited until late in the night on March 31st to give birth to calf number 45......... Mom wrote "happy" on the calendar, so it must have been a long-awaited event. Sam, the bull, got out on April 22nd (two exclamation points, but no follow-up as to the consequences)! One calf born to a heifer developed scours at the end of April and did not want to nurse much in the first two days so he had to be fed bottled milk until he got his appetite back. Because the disease is infectious, more calves came down with it, but apparently Wayne got things under control because none of them died.

Dad and Mom planted early potatoes, turnips, beets and peas on April 17th, more potatoes on May 6th, and then finished the garden except for corn and beans on May 8th. May was a very cold month…..wind, temperatures in the single digits and low 20s, and rain which shifted to snow on the 16th. The cows were in transit……up north first, then south to the big alfalfa pasture, and finally to the draw. The bulls broke out on May 24th!

June was marked by three events: Despite persistent frost, Dad planted his tomatoes on June 3rd and Mom planted corn over again on the 17th; new floor covering and a rug were laid in the porch; and the first crop of hay produced 82 bales on Raymond's. It was noted that the red and white cows were treated for leg problems, and all the cattle were moved up north on June 18th. July's calendar contains no weather information; most of the notations centered on haying. The statistics indicate that during the third week of July, 34 bales were baled north of Wayne's house and 86 on Raymond's, followed by 85 on Colin's, 80 on Raymond's lot, 55 east of Raymond's, and 79 on the northeast forty……that's a lot of hay for the winter months! The cattle occupied Alfred's north of the house, the southeast pasture and the draw.

During the rainy month of August, the cows lived south of Wayne's, on Freddie's, east and north by the house, and up north. The second crop of hay yielded 94 plus 45 bales north on Raymond's. The word for September was rain and then more rain……and then there was the first killing frost on September 29th, followed by 15 degrees and a blizzard on October 1st. Gorgeous weather the fourth week of October wasn't the final word: one inch of snow and a very cold north wind closed out the month. Wayne sold 40 head of cattle on October 16th.

November and December will go down in posterity as containing only one event worth noting: Mom's heart attack on December 23rd and her return home from the hospital on December 29th. Previous to that was her trip to Phyllis's on November 25th. The weather during these two months consisted of beautiful days where the temperatures were in the 30s for the first part of November and then turned very cold (ten degrees below zero) with snow in the last week. The cold weather appeared to carry over into December, resulting in frozen pipes while Mom was in the hospital.

1994 Journal Entry

1994 was ushered in and all that is important is well. Everyone is loving, kind and helpful.

Grandma Rosie hasn't been feeling well this year – she's had a hard time with sinus and other physical problems. I wonder how it will go for her. She is 89 years young!

The summer went by so fast. We had a nice, long, growing season – not too hot and no killing frost until November 1st which is unheard of. We had way too much rain during September, October and November – everything was mud, mud, mud. We couldn't seem to keep the water down in the little basement. And now we're having a pretty hard winter – tremendously cold day after day (30 to 40 degrees below zero) and lots of snow. We haven't had a winter like this for many years.

Shawn and Kevin got married on July 29th. They seem so happy. Joyce quit Weight Watchers and began working with the people at ODC – she enjoys the job very much.

Judy wasn't able to spend very much time at home this summer. But we enjoyed the short visits. Willie came for hunting and both he and Tony got a deer – pretty exciting for them. Zachie hunted last fall and got his deer also.

Jenny is going to Rainy River College in International Falls. She changed her major. It is a much smaller college than Fargo and she says it is friendlier – everyone knows everyone and so she's happy. Chris is working again on his degree at

Alexandria. We don't get to see them very often and miss them very much.

School is so much better for Tony and he seems to be more relaxed – Hannah insists he's her boyfriend and she never changes.

My, how time flies! Willie is a junior; Katie a sophomore; Tony a freshman; and Linsay and Zach are in the 8th grade. In a few years, they'll all be away from home. They are all very active in sports, band, choir, church activities, etc. I pray that each one has accepted Jesus as Savior.

Roz and Jonathan are in the 4th grade and are growing up fast – hard to believe. Little Jena and Hannah are in kindergarten – impossible! Roy and I must be getting old.

1994 Calendar Summary

It was 26 degrees below zero on January 2nd when Bill, the boys and I left the farm after having spent Christmas and New Year's there. It was consistently cold (20 to 40 below; 42 degrees below zero on the 18th to the 20th) during the month until the last week when the thermometer registered above zero. Mom had to go to Fargo for a checkup on January 3rd to the 5th. (The LA earthquake on January 15th registered 6.5 on the Richter Scale.) The brutally cold weather continued into the first two weeks of February……..during that time, a little calf was born on a day when it was 20 degrees below zero. On February 17th, the cold spell broke and it was a beautiful 40 degrees for two or three days……it turned cold again (minus 20 degrees) on February 21st.

March and April: Mom's favorite calendar months! I think she must have seen it as her responsibility to keep track of the calving situation and took great pride in accurately recording the statistics. On March 3rd, Mom returned from Toledo to be greeted with beautiful 40 - degree weather and a significant decrease in the amount of snow that was on the ground when she left. The second week of March saw temperatures plummeting to below zero and they remained that way for the rest of the month. The calves began arriving on March 12th in the cold and snow. For once, Mom's information is a little confusing. She recorded the individual births of 15 calves for March, but there also appears a kind of summary at the end: 4 bulls, 4 heifers, 3 heifers, 1 heifer, 1 bull, 2 bulls, and 10 heifers for a total of 25 calves. So, the two sets of numbers don't add up and it's not certain how many calves were born during the month. Of the total – whichever one is correct – one little darling, born in the wee hours of a cold, snowy morning, was brought into the house for some tender loving care. We think he survived, but on April 3rd, an "older" calf died, and it might have been he. On March 12th, the mother of a red calf with horns died, leaving behind "Orphie." Then, on March 29th, the calf of Number 13 cow died, leaving her motherless. Three days later, Mom recorded that Orphie is sucking Number 13, so things worked out for the orphan calf and the motherless mom!

Weather comments for April: Wet snow…partly cloudy….beautiful day…..highs in the 50s…..blizzard with 3 to 4 inches of snow….cold and sunny. Three heifers were tagged and nine calves were born, including one little fellow named "Tubby." Mom proclaimed April 25th as the day when calving season was officially over. Dad planted potatoes on April 20th and Mom peas and onions on the 22nd.

May brought chicken pox to Rozie and Hannah. Jenny departed for Toledo, where she would spend the summer staying with us and babysitting for some friends of ours. Rain fell but it didn't dominate the month so that potato planting day was able to take place on May 14th, and some more of the garden was planted. The drought continued into June, so that everyone was waiting for rain. One good thing that comes out of dry weather is haying: 37 alfalfa bales were baled at Ed's and 24 up north at Raymond's….. "good, good hay." Mom planted onions on June 7th. Sam and Adolph escaped on June 5th, and this decision on their part may have contributed to Sam's fate of being sent to Adolph Severson's a few days later.

The black cows spent their days with the heifers around the farm, and the rest lived in the draw up north, where one cow had the misfortune of being killed by lightning.

During the month of July, 460 bales of hay were prepared for winter consumption: 114 bales of hay at the house; 86 bales up north; 42 south of the house; 54 at Raymond's house; 95 at Raymond's up north; and 98 bales of timothy. (The individual numbers add up to 489, which differs from Mom's total by 29 bales.) The cattle were all together up north where one cow died from unreported causes. Mom indicated that Jon stayed with them on the farm while I attended a conference in Minneapolis. The most important event of the month was Shawn and Kevin's wedding.

August produced 51 bales of hay for a grand total of 521 hay bales for the summer (again, the numbers are slightly different when one adds up the individual counts, but plus or minus ten bales doesn't appear to be significant). Haying went well, despite the overabundance of rain.

September brought a terrible storm with six and a half to seven inches of rain and jagged hail while I was home. The cattle were way up north at this time and cow Number 31 had her calf in the early morning hours of the storm. Hot weather (70 to 80 degrees) followed the rainy part of the month. Mom and Dad took two trips to Thief River and a weekend trip to Duluth where they were met with rain and cold. They saw one impressive ship, but there was not much fall color to enjoy. There must have been an occasion for gift giving because Mom made a note that a scarf was given to me, a picture to Shawn and Sharon, and a cooler to Pam and Wayne (a notable variety of gifts, I might add).

"Absolutely gorgeous weather" marked the days of October, with the first real frost arriving on October 20th (26 degrees) and a skiff of snow on the 23rd. Two events were noteworthy during this month: Hannah's hand-picked bouquet of dandelions and Phyllis and her family's weekend visit at the end of the month.

Opening deer season weekend in November was cold and rainy. Mom noted that Willie went home on the 7th, so he (but not Bill and the other two boys) must have been home for hunting. Wayne separated the calves and cows and began feeding them hay, although there was still some pasture for them to eat. A period of snow, rain and blizzard conditions on the weekend of the 18th was followed by some mild weather which continued into December, although there is no indication of how long that weather lasted and what followed. Mom did record that it was so beautiful on December 1st that she washed clothes and dried them on the line! Nothing else appeared on the December calendar.

1995 Journal Entries

May

Much has happened since I wrote last. The school year is swiftly coming to a close. Katie went to the prom with Jared – they have become good friends. She passed her swimming exam this winter and now she works as a lifeguard at the pool.

Jenny has definitely made plans to be a nanny out east for the next year. She had an excellent year at college but this is something that she has wanted to do and felt that now is the time – she'll be working in New Jersey and leaves the fourth of June. She'll be gone a long time, and now we'll really miss her. I do pray that God will bless her and that she will be a blessing to her new friends also (this is almost like having Judy leave to go out East many years ago).

Chris is graduating on May 25th. He is staying in Alexandria for the summer so that he's close to the job market – at least that is the plan now. I really love Chris and I'm glad that he's not afraid to give his old Grandma a hug and a kiss when I see him which is not very often.

Judy said that Willie is really into yard work this year – going to make some "big bucks." He's making plans to attend a Bible Camp in New York – I pray that his interest in God flourishes.

Both Zach and Tony are being confirmed this spring. All of the children are as lovely as ever and are growing up in the nurture and admonition of the Lord – thanks to their Christian parents who are guiding them to Jesus Christ as their Savior.

Mom had an excellent winter. She's been traveling a lot, visiting whenever she can.

Sharon is fighting the cancer which surfaced in her lung this winter. We are thanking God for what he has done for her and what he will do. What would we do if we didn't have Jesus to go to with our problems and our despair? He is such a faithful friend – praise him.

The little calves aren't doing so well this spring – several have died. Wayne feels it is the disgustingly poor hay. It was so wet last summer that most of it is practically useless – filler but no nutrients.

Wayne and Pam are remodeling their house and finally fixing the lower level. So much work but it is really nice.

July 31

Well, we made it! Celebrated our 50th in June and now the kids have given us a trip to Estes Park, Colorado. The mountains are wondrous and the rivers, lakes, and valleys all add up to great scenery! Surely the works of the Lord are great and He is to be worshipped in awe. We are having a good time together.

As it turned out, the thin mountain air didn't agree with me. I got really sick so we left a little early – it's the "berries." The rest did a lot of mountain climbing, etc. I found out that Judy and her family drove up to Pikes Peak, which was a destination for all of us. I'm glad but I know I spoiled the vacation, at least for Pam and Wayne and the others who were with us.

The rest of the summer went by as usual. So much to do. At least it wasn't so wet and rainy. The garden was good – tomatoes were scrumptious; corn, potatoes, cucumbers, etc. were plentiful.

October

The weather is gorgeous most of the time – fall colors everywhere and the leaves are slow to fall. Mom, Inez, Irene, Evie and I drove to Oklahoma – had such a good trip. We stayed just long enough not to wear out our welcome. On Friday night, Phyllis took all of us to the race track – now that was something different and a lot of fun. I didn't win much money but didn't lose any either.

School is going fine for the kids most of the time. Report cards will come out soon and they will tell the tale.

November

Oh, what a long winter this will be! The first week of November we had six inches of snow – of course, the cold came with it. And despite Roy's predictions that it would all melt, more followed. The deer hunters earned their deer, for sure – wading in calf-high snow and posting in freezing temperatures. But they scored pretty good.

On November 20th, I had a second heart attack! Dr. Herseth sent me to Fargo and there on the 24th I had a double bypass. Like one visitor said, "It will be no picnic but you'll make it." And he was so right in both ways.

1995 Calendar Summary

January and February were cold months, for the most part. Except for the last three days of January when Mom said that it was "very nice" and a week toward the end of February when the snow was melting, temperatures settled in the 20s and 30s below zero. It snowed six inches in the middle of January, and the water pipes froze. The heifers got in with the cows, and one cow aborted her calf. February also saw cattle fraternization……..this time the calves and the bulls decided to keep company. Mom substitute taught for Karen a couple of days.

March......Mom's most prolific news month, usually dominated by the calving situation, but this time, she reported news about the crows first: On March 5th, we learn that the crows have been around for a while, some all winter. The robins also returned on March 19th. On March 8th, it was 25 degrees below zero and the water in the house froze; it opened a week later. The sewer also thawed out. Seventeen calves were born during the month, many in the early morning. Mom had a doctor's appointment on March 8th when it was 25 below.

Twenty-three calves were born in April, including "Little Red" who died. The good news was that "Little Blackie", who was born in the wee hours of a very cold April 1st morning, started sucking the next day, much to Mom's relief. The first two weeks of April were cold (0-10 degrees) and stormy with three plus inches of snow on the 11th. The weather turned mild so that the snow melted, and Mom was able to plant onions on the 24th. The month ended with a skiff of snow on the 27th. Mom diligently kept track of her blood pressure during this month.

During the "very cold and wet" month of May (froze hard on the 21st), Adolph was romping with the cows and

Tubby had her calf. The garage was painted the week of the 14th. Mom, along with Grandma Rosie and Rozie left for Toledo on the 31st; they returned home on June 8th to find everything looking good. Two calves were born and the cows were separated from the bulls while they were gone. It froze slightly on June 7th and turned very hot and dry the third week. The month ended with a great deal of rain and cool weather. Phyllis, Pat and Jessie, as well as Natalie and Tootsie visited the last part of June. Mom wrote down "Baby Hannah" with no explanation, so it's unclear what happened to Hannah in June.

Wayne started haying on July 3rd........106 bales on Freddy's on the 15th; 73 on Raymond's field up north; 137 on Ed's timothy; and 88 bales up north by the grade. The cows and both bulls were together again. The days were hot in the middle of the month and wet the last couple of weeks. Mom and Dad left for the trip out west with the family on July 29th......6 "bells", Mom wrote.....and returned home on August 5th to find two new baby calves. August weather was simply gorgeous: hot days and very cool nights.....no hint of frost. On August 28th, Mom washed clothes and went to Thief River where they had the oil changed in the blue car. Inside the pocket of the calendar was a list of hay bales for the month of August: 42 on Ed's alfalfa; 41 on Raymond's field by the house; 16 by the road to Wayne's; 60 on Fred's timothy; and 33 out south. The total for July and August - for 1995 - was 596 bales of hay.

September's weather was variable: one to two inches of rain fell on the 5th, followed by frost on the 7th; it was very warm the week of the 11th, but turned cold (30s and 20s) with killing frost and two to three inches of snow on the 18th; and the month ended with beautiful weather. During the cold spell, Mom washed clothes and went to Thief River with Dad. She left for Oklahoma on the 26th and returned home on October 1st to rain and a guilty verdict for OJ Simpson. The second week of October produced an Indian summer followed by a rainy week. Liz Patberg died on the 16th. On October 19th, a dinner shower was held for Theresa whose daughter, Jackie, was born on July 13th, Mom's birthday. Wayne separated the cattle on the 28th.

Mom had a second heart attack on November 20th. She was "shipped" to Fargo on the 22nd and had surgery on the 24th. The weather report consisted of a snow storm at the beginning of the month which dropped six to seven inches of snow in one day and continued for several days. Wayne started feeding the cattle during the storm and conducted pregnancy tests on six heifers on the 18th. Mom wrote "No. 12 open" (I don't know what that means.)

"Snow! Snow! Snow and sub-zero temperatures"........

December began with a bang! Mom came home from the hospital on December 5th. Christmas brought mild temperatures. Bill, Judy and the boys arrived on December 23rd to enjoy a white Christmas.

Chapter 5
1996 – 1999

(1996 journal entries and calendar summary, 1997 journal entry and calendar summary, 1998 journal entries and calendar summary, 1999 calendar summary)

Do not be afraid, for I am with you; I will bring your children from the east and gather you from the west. I will say to the north, "Give them up!" and to the south, "Do not hold them back." Bring my sons from afar and my daughters from the ends of the earth – everyone who is called by name, whom I created for my glory, whom I formed and made.
Isaiah 43: 5-7

1996 Journal Entries

January 11

I'm recuperating slowly, but surely. Everyone predicts that

I will be a new woman – I hope it will all be worth it. II Chronicles 2:15, "Be not afraid……the fight is not yours but God's" – Praise him!

Everyone was home for Christmas – what a good time we had together! We had Christmas Eve at Pam and Wayne's house. Katie, Linsay, and Rozie were battling strep-throat so later on, guess what? Tony contracted it and now two weeks later, Zach is down. I wonder how many more. We'll see.

Everyone has been so good to me – washing clothes, cleaning, and all the other "good stuff" that goes with living. Roy did the cooking and dishes the first couple of weeks I was home – he also vacuumed!

On New Year's Day all of the healthy people rode snowcats across country to Sportsman's Lodge north of Baudette. The weather cooperated and they all had a good time driving and riding. The rest of us rode in cars.

The winter has been pretty – lots of pure white snow that has created huge hills in the yard.

February

Not much news. I feel very good except for the uncomfortable soreness in my chest and my leg keeps swelling. I praise God for his love and mercy – He is so faithful!

The second week of February Gayle had classes in Fargo and I went with her – we were gone four days. While she was in school I read, crocheted, walked, etc. and the days weren't that long. One evening Chris and Mandy came to see us – Jared was over one evening and we went to see "Father of the Bride II" another evening.

A little calf was born on the 22nd – a nice big bull calf. I pray he'll make it (He did!). Another calf was born a week later.

March 15

No more calves. Winter is still here but it is losing its grip – much snow but days between are lovely.

May 15

The snow is just now disappearing – a long, long winter. Easter has passed and yesterday was Mother's Day. No bare ground for the Easter egg hunt but we had a lovely time together. Roy hid the eggs in the sheds, Quonset and snowbanks!

Mother's Day – the weather was just perfect! The kids all came over and we had a work day – flower beds dug up, yard cleaned, plumbing fixed and bathrooms given a face lift. New window, ceiling fixed and carpet laid – oh, what fun! God bless each and every one! How I do love them all – from the oldest to the littlest.

Calving is very slow – about one half done.

Sharon is doing so well. Praise God for His goodness. Our little Bible study is almost done for this book. I hope we can continue more when fall comes.

June 1

Inez has cancer surgery on her breast on Tuesday. I so pray that it is God's perfect will that it will be a success.

I had my six-month appointment in Fargo yesterday. Dr. Dickson had nothing to say that I already didn't know. My heart is doing fine, but the healing process in my chest is slow. Maybe the pain in my chest, as well as in my leg and ankle, will never really go away – oh well, I'm thankful that the things that are bothering me won't necessarily kill me.

Tonight Mom and I leave for Toledo for Willie's graduation (I'm excited but apprehensive, as well.)

July

We got home from Toledo in good shape with many memories of a wonderful time. So many of our family were there, as well as Pat. It was good to see him. A lot has happened since then. I had a mammogram and it showed two spots – had a sonogram and then a biopsy on July 25th. The one was just a mass but the other one they sent away so now I'm waiting for the results of that test.

The Loewens have left and there's a real void in the church. I really miss them.

Jonathan came on Thursday. He's such a nice little guy but so quiet – what is he thinking about? Judy, Bill, Willie and Zach are coming next week. The Pearson reunion is next weekend. Judy has worked very hard on the event and I pray that many will come.

<u>Note</u>: The Pearson reunion in August was a huge success, from the large number of family members who attended to the t-shirts designed by Chris that said, "Pearsons…..the Fun Bunch" (accompanied by a picture of the stoic American Gothic couple holding pitchforks). A good time was had by all, including Dad's cousin, Orlin Pearson, and his daughter from Minneapolis.

September

Another summer is past – fall begins tomorrow. Today is a real autumn day – so overcast and damp, almost to the point of rain. Needless to say, it's not a very pleasant day.

The Years Come and Go

Willie is going to start classes at Ohio State University – I think he leaves today. I pray for him as I do for all my grandchildren.

The Pearson reunion seemed to be a success. We held it at Bemis Hill and I was really glad we were there because it rained during the noon meal. Later on the sun came out, and I think that everyone had a good time.

August and September have been good months. The sun has shone a lot and there hasn't been a frost yet. The garden was pretty good despite the poor beginning. The kids are back in school and all are satisfied with their teachers. Even Tony seems to be "hacking it" – he picked up his new snocat yesterday and was all smiles. He'll have to keep working to pay for that "hunk of a toy."

Grandma Rosie was sick about a month or so ago but she is doing quite well now – 92 years young in a couple of weeks.

Inez has about three treatments left and then they'll give her an MRI to see if they have done any good. Sharon also has another MRI soon. They both are in good spirits and trust God for their future. Of course, we all pray that the cancer will go away.

We have started our Bible Study again with Sue as our leader. Our book this fall is "Lord, Change Me" – we've had a couple of good discussions. Pam, Julie, Gayle and Annette have joined the group and it's wonderful to have their input.

October

We spent a weekend with Cy. He invited all of Norma's family to come and stay at the cabin – we really had a good time together.

What a beautiful fall! The weather is perfect most days. Roy is finishing the hay hauling, and each day goes by without anything bad happening.

Winter

The winter began early and was the worst in many years – very cold most of the time and we were always working with snow. The kids had many vacation days from school. In places the snow didn't disappear until way out in May, but we made it through in good shape.

Sharon and Ron were married in June and they all seem to be happy.

1996 Calendar Summary

Mild weather marked the first couple of weeks in January (20 degrees), but then it turned cold (minus 20 degrees to minus 40 degrees), and all the water froze. Snow fell for several days. Wayne shipped 14 calves and one "open" heifer on January 18th; the skinny cow died on the 25th. Three hundred and fifty gallons of propane were delivered on January 23rd.

It was 47 degrees below zero with a high of 31 degrees on February 1st! A heat wave with temperatures in the 20s and 30s with some rain lasted for a couple of weeks, and then very wintry conditions set in again the last couple of days of the month. Dad went to Thief River by himself on a day when it was 35 below, and both Mom and Dad went a week later after it had warmed up. Two calves were born and survived the frigid temperatures.

March came in like a calm lion – continued cold but sunny. The temperatures ranged from a low of minus 35 degrees to a high of five degrees above zero. Mom labeled the third week of March "beautiful"; the fourth week "clear and cold"; and the last week "sunshine and beautiful but a raw cold wind." On March 29th, it was thirty below and the water froze in the kitchen and porch. Six calves were born in the month. Mom and Dad went to Thief River three times, once for Dad's appointment and once to grocery shop.

April brought a mixture of weather……..snow, rain, sunshine, cold, beautiful, and a very nasty "terrible mess" on the last couple of days. Seventeen calves were born in April. The Sandhill cranes arrived on April 8th.

Three calves were born in May, one with pneumonia who later died. Mom made a point of declaring that there was no frost on May 5th. Two newsworthy items: A new sofa was purchased on May 14th and the garden was finished on the 30th. However, Dad had to replant the potatoes on June 18th because the month had been extremely wet. On June 26th, the temperature plummeted to 30 degrees but there was no frost. The bulls got out on June 1st, and the cows were moved from the southwest pasture to the draw two weeks later. A new bull joined the bovine family on June 20th. Mom noted that Leroy planted Sigurd's on June 13th, followed by the finishing of Freddy's and Mike's land. Mom and Dad and Grandma Rosie paid a visit to Toledo the first part of June for Will's high school graduation.

Mom's July calendar is hard to interpret. Every day from July 14th to July 24th she has written down names with no clue as to why they occupy space on her calendar. The names are as follows: Sue and family; Inez and Sharon; Fred and Bev; Teresa, Jackie and family; Millie; Phyllis and family; Irene and Richard; Evie and family; Annette and family; Mom; and Gerry, Mitzi, and family. Other noteworthy items include Katie and Linsay on a plane on the 17th, Jon getting on a plane on the 25th and Jenny coming home on the 29th. A calf was given a shot on the 12th, and the cattle were moved to the draw on the 27th. It rained four to five inches on July 18th. Mom also tracked her blood pressure during this month.

Judy, Bill and family came home on August 1st for the Pearson family reunion at Bemis Hill on the 3rd. Bill and Willie went back to Toledo on the 8th, while Judy, Zach and Jon stayed until the 15th. The cattle were in the pasture north of the house and were then moved to the southeast pasture. A new calf was born on August 25th. On August 16th, Mom noted that the weather was warm, hot and dry. She stayed with Grandma Rosie on the 21st to the 23rd. During that time, lightning killed a yearling. Mom and Dad went to Thief River twice that month, once for Mom's eye exam and a hair appointment.

Beautiful weather characterized the first part of September when the cattle were grazing in the southwest pasture. Mom stayed with Grandma Rosie, and went to Grand Forks with Inez. In October, Mom and Grandma Rosie celebrated Grandma Rosie's birthday by going to Baudette to visit Cy. During the beautiful Indian summer weather (highs in the 40s and 50s) a little calf was born and Wayne sold nine cows. The weather turned very cold (high winds, temperatures ranging from highs in the 20s to a low of 12 degrees) the last week. Bulls from Gurney's arrived on the 29th, and another little calf was born a couple of days later.

November began with two calves being born in snowy cold weather when the water system froze. The second week brought beautiful weather with the shipping of two calves. A calf was born during the week of terribly cold weather which continued through Thanksgiving. The only entry on the December calendar mentioned the exceptionally mild weather and lots of snow during the first two weeks. Mom, Joyce, Gayle and Pam went to the Cities for their annual weekend with Judy.

1997 Journal Entry

This winter is just the opposite from last year......mild weather and not too much snow so far. The cows are really enjoying the mild temperatures as are we.

Katie is going to UMD at Duluth. She hasn't really decided on a major yet but there's time. Willie is in his second year at OSU – I think he is also undecided. They are still young and God is busy shaping them both.

Jenny stayed out East again – she loves it there. She'll graduate sometime at the end of 1998 with a specialized degree in therapy of some kind. She expects to graduate cum laude! I wonder if she'll come back to Minnesota. I miss her but do want her to be happy – her dad said the other day that he misses her cookies!

Chris and Mandy are still in Alexandria – not married which depresses me, but I hope they'll do it soon. Chris has had a few problems which I think are being resolved. I surely pray for him, as I do for all of my grandchildren.

It's hard to think of Tony as a senior this year and will also be leaving us behind. He's happy this year with school; he quit hockey, and took up snocat racing with Carter Diesen – that is just up his alley.

Zachie is working very diligently in maintaining a high average in his junior year. I think he would like to go to an air force school, and one has to have consistent high marks to get in.

Linsay is also a junior. School is not one of her priorities – does all right but doesn't strive to be the best she can be. She's an excellent little basketball player. She had mono last fall just when they were choosing the A team so she was left out, but the coach uses her often. I love to watch her play.

Jonathan continues to be an excellent student. He is so gifted on the violin and also plays the trumpet in band – as sweet as ever.

Rozie, Hannah and Jena like school and do well. Hannah and Jena take piano lessons and Rozie plays in the band.

Sharon and Ron are expecting a baby in March. We are all so excited – it's been a long time since we had a baby in the house. Shawn and Kevin bought a cute little house of their own and they keep busy with this and that.

I love all these beautiful young people so much and pray that all of them have made the commitment to accept Jesus Christ as part of their lives. What a joy each one is – I'm so blessed!

In January, Roy and I went by train to Judy and Bill's and spent a few days with them. While in Toledo, we took the plane and flew to Florida for a couple of days – what an experience! This was all a Christmas present from them! I've always had a yen to try flying but never had the courage to do so. The clouds and the sky are beautiful up there – God is in his heavens!

<u>Note</u>: Mom, Dad, Jonathan and I spent three days in Vero Beach. We had a fabulous time building sand castles on the beach, enjoying the dolphins at Sea World, and feasting on delicious oranges. What I had in mind was that a trip to Florida would become a yearly event for Mom and Dad, so they could find some respite from the cold Minnesota winter.

But, there was to be none of that.......Dad decided that once was enough, even though he enjoyed himself a great deal. I think that Mom could have been convinced to repeat the experience, but she couldn't go without Dad.

1997 Calendar Summary

January began with temperatures in the 30s, turned colder for the middle of the month, and ended with very nice weather that extended into February. Wayne sold 19 calves to Dwaine. Judy spent a stormy and cold January week on the farm. February was marked by cold (minus 20 degrees) and sunny weather for most of the month.

Balmy weather – very windy but sunny – dressed the first week of March, followed by beautiful days interspersed with some very cold temperatures (minus 20 to 25 degrees). Katie's basketball team lost the championship. Seven calves were born, one to the horned cow and another to Number 34, which died a week later. Nine calves were born in April. A very bad storm occurred during the second week when the water system froze and people snocatted to Bemis Hill, despite the cold. April ended with beautiful weather.

May's week by week weather report: very rainy, very cold and wet, cold and rainy, and beautiful weather....... it snowed one day. A little calf was born at the beginning of the month. Nikki Nordby's wedding was on May 17th, and Katie's high school graduation was on the 31st. Bill, Jon and Judy came home for her graduation (70 degrees). Goldfinches, hummingbirds and Baltimore Orioles were out in full bird force on May 21st.

June brought very warm and dry weather (80 degrees one day) for the first two weeks and then rain for the remainder of the month. The bulls were let out on a lovely June 1st day when the cows were grazing in the draw; they were later moved to the south pasture and finished out the month east of the house. Mom and Dad left for Michigan on June 26th and returned on July 7th to be greeted by hot and very humid weather with quite a bit of rain. Blueberries started to ripen on July 13th, and the season was in full swing by the next week when Mom and Dad frequently filled their pails. Three hundred and seventy-two hay bales dotted the fields by the end of the month: 138 bales from Raymond's, 150 on Lind's, 30 way up north, and 14 by the house (doesn't quite add up, but those are the figures on the calendar). The cattle were moved to the southwest pasture where a little calf was born. In August, the cattle moved around a great deal: north pasture to the draw, then to the east pasture and south pasture, ending the month in the east pasture and the draw. August was a hot month, but the heat didn't prevent Dad from painting the house white.

Dad continued to paint in September, this month the garage and shed doors. The weather was beautiful with a slight frost on September 18th. Two little calves were born on the 19th of September and five during the month of October, one to the gray cow with no ears. An October thunderstorm produced lots of rain which turned to three inches of snow and then another two inches a week later. It was 15 degrees on the morning of October 26th……..four days later the snow was melting. The cattle occupied the pasture east of the house.

Rain and snow forced the calves into the barn for a few days in November, until the weather turned mild (20 to 40 degrees) when they were let out to enjoy beautiful days for the rest of the month. Tony shot a big buck and Willie a smaller one during the opening deer season weekend. Mom caught a bad cold which lasted four days.

The very mild temperatures (highs in the 20s and lows of 15 and 10 degrees) carried over into December and escalated the third week (36 degrees and sunshine) only to fall into the low teens over Christmas. The water froze when it got down to minus 15 degrees. Wayne shipped 14 calves with Dwaine. Mom went to Minneapolis with Pam, Gayle and Joyce …….they met me for our annual weekend.

A word about the 1997 calendar……..each month featured helpful farmhouse hints, farm business tips, and farm reference data (probably from the 50s). One of the housekeeping hints strongly advised women to not allow their household to become a mess because it takes so long to straighten it up, so "make a habit of returning everything to its proper place immediately after use." I wonder if Mom smiled when she read this.

1998 Journal Entries

February

Very little snow and unbelievable temperatures – upper 20s, 30s and 40s in the daytime and low 20s at night. On Valentine's Day it rained!

Wayne's family; Joyce, Rod and Jena; and Gayle and Tony went skiing at Boyne. They have an annual date with Judy and Bill and family and friends. This year they roasted Wayne for his 40th birthday. They had a great time but Judy fell and broke her knee and pulled ligaments, so she was in great pain. She'll be hobbling on crutches for a long time.

Note: Wayne's roast was great fun! Our boys had bought a little garter snake from a pet shop in Toledo and brought it to the Boyne house where they presented it to Wayne during the roast. Wayne's pathological fear of snakes went into full gear, and the boys had to put the little guy back in his box. When we returned to Toledo, they decided to return the snake to the pet shop but couldn't find him. We searched the house and finally gave up. We never did find that little snake, and I hoped that he located an exit from the house and lived happily ever after.

March

The winter continues to be exceptionally nice – mild most of the time with a minimum amount of snow. Snocatters don't appreciate it but we do.

Spring came very early – most of the time, beautiful weather. The crocuses and daffodils are so pretty and the tulips aren't too far behind. Roy planted the potatoes the Monday after Easter and the garden not long after that, but then it got so dry the germination was slow.

Grandma Rozie has been at Sheltering Oaks for a year now. She says it's okay but some days she wonders why she's there because she feels so good. Ninety-three years old – the Lord continues to give her strength for each day! I pray for her and also for Pat (Bill's father) who's hanging in there but not doing so well. Grandma says she got "out of jail" this week so now she can spend some time away from there if she wants to.

May

Linsay and Tony both had dates for the prom and they were gorgeous! What would I do without my grandchildren to dote on? Now Tony graduates in May. Judy, Bill and the boys are all coming for the weekend. Jenny is coming too so the whole bunch will be around. Isn't that great!

Little Seth John was born on April 9th. What a little darling – 20 inches long and 7 pounds, 15 ounces. He looks just like Ron.

Everyone is fine – getting a little older and a little wiser. The school year is quickly drawing to a close – spring programs and band concerts are over. Hannah had her piano recital (she did very well) and the only thing left is the last day of school.

August

Judy and her family drove up for Tony's graduation in June. His graduation party was very nice – outside with a "big top" for protection against adverse weather. Then, Judy and Jon came back for two weeks. It's been a great summer – on the go at all times! Rozie went back with Judy and Jon and will come home in a couple of weeks.

The summer is almost gone – where did it go so fast? It

has been quite wet, July especially – raining almost every day. Needless to say, not much haying got done.

The garden isn't so good – too wet for such a long period of time. But the flowers are beautiful, and it looks as if the corn is going to produce well.

Katie and Linsay have both been lifeguarding – Katie also works part time at the Legion restaurant. Tony has been working at the Cenex C Store and mowing some lawns – also doing a lot of golfing and fishing. The younger ones have had Bible School, Bible Camp and other activities to keep them busy and content. School soon starts again and then they'll be pretty busy.

Grandma Rozie has not been too well. She's finally showing her age – 94 in October!

Phyllis' Pat died in June. Not so old – 69, I think. She'll miss him dreadfully but she'll make it. Her family is so considerate of her.

Freddie has had a tough time. He has been treated for prostate cancer and the latest report is that the cancer is gone – another prayer answered! His back and legs are very bad and hopefully they too can be corrected. Bev smashed her hand at work very badly – a huge press came down and hit it hard, so she has been in a lot of pain also.

1998 Calendar Summary

January and February were generally unseasonably warm with temperatures ranging from 20 degrees to 40 degrees and rain instead of snow. There were a couple of days at the beginning of January where it was very cold (minus 20 degrees); similarly, it was 10 degrees below zero for two days at the beginning of February. Mom called February "a remarkable month." A calf was aborted on January 2nd. Mom and Dad left for Toledo on the 12:55 a.m. train from Grand Forks on January 8th.

The first comment to appear on the March calendar was Mom's statement that this was "the cloudiest winter since 1982, an El Nino year." Despite her assessment, there appeared to have been a few days that brought beautiful sunshine. Temperatures hovered around 10 degrees below zero, with high winds the second week of the month, and rose as the month went on. Fourteen calves were born: the first one's mother was Big Red, and Mom thinks that one was born to Number 9th; one little guy was brought into the house for tender loving care. Two calves were born to Number 7. April brought seven more calves plus 52 little yellow chicks. It was a beautiful month…..warm and dry for the most part (79 degrees one day). Mom had her eyes checked and went to Thief River for a doctor's appointment. She must have been into meal planning: tater tots and leftovers, potatoes and roast, sauerkraut and hot dogs, and pork chops.

In May, Mom paid the insurance company $280.70. She prepared a roast, stuffed peppers, soup, and omelets for at least four meals during the month. Four calves were born, and the cows lived in the draw. She had her hair done on May 18th. The first week of June was very cold with a light frost, and heavy rains fell on the 19th. The cows were grazing up north and were then taken to the draw with the bulls and young stock where they stayed for a couple of weeks before being taken to the south pasture; a calf was born. A field was done on June 5th, and Fred's field was completed on the 11th.

The cattle were moved to the draw on July 1st and then to the east pasture, to the draw again, and finally up north. Thirty-two hay bales were baled on July 13th and Raymond's big field was baled on the 21st. Judy arrived for a sojourn on the farm on the 17th. August produced hot and dry weather (80 to 90 degrees) which allowed for the baling to be completed on Lisell's…….200 bales in all.

"Beautiful weather – blue skies and white clouds – gorgeous foliage……thank you, God." So begins September's calendar. On September 6th, the temperature was down to 36 degrees, and on the 10th, it was 90 degrees. It was once again a moveable feast for the cattle. A little calf was fortunate to be born on a day that was very dry and warm.

In contrast, there was a lot of thunder and rain during a time in October when Mom and Dad went to Duluth to visit Katie. It froze hard on October 2nd, a day before the cattle were fed; two week later, it was 43 degrees with sunshine. Mom washed clothes twice.

November produced a snowstorm with five to six inches of snow, followed by ten more inches a week later. A little calf was born with no mother (?) and another was born in the glorious sunshine of Thanksgiving week. Mom and Dad took Bill and Jon to Thief River to catch a plane home to Toledo…..no mention was made of whether they shot any deer. December began on a beautiful weather note, and it didn't turn cold until the 18th (minus 20 degrees). Bill, the boys and I went to the farm for Christmas and enjoyed a very cold week (minus 20 degrees)…..we left on the 30th.

1999 Calendar Summary

It was so cold the first week of January (minus 30 degrees) that the water and sewer froze up and didn't thaw out until the 16th when it warmed up to 30 degrees above zero. On the 17th, a mild snowstorm dropped six to eight inches of snow, and the temperatures remained above zero for the rest of the month. Mom and Dad went to Thief River and then to Fargo with Gayle. Mild temperatures began the month of February, but it quickly turned cold (minus 18 degrees) and then, just as quickly became mild (50 degrees), very cold (minus 20), and very nice (40s above).

The weather was beautiful with "good snow for snocatting" the first week in March when I was home. It turned cold the next week (10 below) with five inches of snow, followed by rain and nasty weather the last week. Eleven calves were born during this cold weather.......one died. Eleven more calves were born in April, but the big calf died, a factor that saddened Mom a great deal. For the first time that Mom could remember, there was no egg hunt on Easter because of the snow.

May brought beautiful weather the first part of the month, followed by cold and rain (three and a half inches) and a three-day frost at the end of the month. June was a rainy month with "tornados all around." The cattle were moved from the south to the north to the pasture by the barn and settled in the draw the first part of July. Mom and Dad went to Toledo for a visit. It rained hard the first part of July, but then the weather cooperated so that Wayne was able to cut hay on Linds and bale on the 19th. Mom wrote: "Hen set, new eggs." The August calendar was blank. The September calendar consisted of one entry: Beautiful month....one hard frost....everything still growing. October and November were blank. The first two weeks of December were very mild with temperatures in the 30s and 40s and no snow. Mom hung clothes on the line to dry. She left for the annual mother-daughter and daughter-in-law weekend in Minneapolis on December 3rd. It snowed two inches on December 16th and turned very cold (minus 20 degrees) right before Christmas.

Chapter 6
1996

From "Mom, Share your Life with Me"

(Mom answered questions in a journal Joyce asked her to complete in 1996. Instead of presenting the information in the question-answer format that appeared in the journal, I have re-arranged it into a narrative.)

Do not be afraid, for I have ransomed you. I have called you by name; you are mine. When you go through deep water, I will be with you. When you go through rivers of difficulty, you will not drown. When you walk through the fire of oppression, you will not be burned up; the flames will not consume you.
Isaiah 43: 1-2

I was born at my parents' home in Pencer, Minnesota on July 13, 1925. A midwife delivered me – I think her name was Mrs. Denault. My mother's name was Rosalyn Tina Zorn. Her father's name was August, and her mother's name was Mary Roggo. My father's name was Arthur Albert Gustav Clasen, born to Fredrick Clasen and Marie Yeske. Rosalyn Zorn was born in Wabbasso, Minnesota on October 5, 1904, and Arthur Clasen was born in Superior, Wisconsin on March 28, 1898.

Franklin Delano Roosevelt was president when I was born. He won four presidential elections....a record for our country. The country was in very bad shape then – depression, people out of work – but FDR implemented a program that pulled us out. I voted for FDR in 1944, when I was 18. Roy still believes that Roosevelt was the best president this country has ever had, and I can't disagree with him.

I have ten brothers and sisters: Norma Ruth – May 21, 1924; Irene Alma – January 12, 1927; Evelyn Ann – November 21, 1928; Inez Grace – August 29, 1930; Phyllis Lucille – November 22, 1932; Geraldine Deno – July 10, 1935; Fredrick August – February 18, 1937; Mildred Muriel – September 29, 1939; Imogene Rosalyn – October 21, 1941; and Sharon Louise – March 21, 1943. Phyllis's nickname was Moptop, called this by Dad because of her wonderful head of hair. Imogene was known as Tootsie and Sharon was Muggsy. I feel very comfortable calling them by their nicknames to this day. My nickname was Maggie. I don't know where it came from and, as I grew older, it wasn't used very much.

The Years Come and Go

Daddy's main occupation was a farmer. He worked as a woodsman at the Northwest Angle with his Dad. In later years, he bought a truck and supplemented his earnings by hauling milk for the farmers to the creamery in Roseau. He did this for a number of years. Mom worked as a pastry cook at the café in Roseau in her later years. She was an excellent baker and cook.

While I was small, my Grandpa and Grandma Clasen lived across the road. I thought they had the loveliest house in the world.....was always so neat and clean and cool in the summer. I have so many pleasant memories of that place – big spruce trees to climb, animals of every kind, the whippoorwill, and the pond that froze over in the spring after the snow had gone so we could shoe skate.

Grandma was a matronly lady as were all the grandmas in those days. She had beautiful hands. Grandma Clasen lived with Dad and Mom the last years of her life. I was married and had my own home by the time she moved in. For a time, Grandpa Clasen was a traveling salesman for the Watkin's Company. Oh, the most wonderful aromas came from his little storage shed (my favorite were the little round gum balls)! Grandpa Clasen had reddish hair and a big, thick mustache. I don't remember my Grandpa Zorn.

I never knew most of my aunts very well as they lived far from us. Aunt Alma and Aunt Lydia always seemed so kind.

Aunt Ruth lived with Grandpa and Grandma so we knew her quite well. She liked to make May baskets and bring them over, put them by the door, and then run away and hide. Her baskets were made from whatever was available, but always included fudge and divinity which were her specialties. Aunt Ruth took me to my first movie, "Laurel and Hardy." She had such a hard life. I loved her very much and when I think of her, my heart goes out to her. I think my favorite uncle was Uncle Willis – what a great guy he was! He lived in Devils Lake, North Dakota, and was married to Aunt Lydia. He died of bone cancer, and shortly after his death, Aunt Lydia died.

As far as my cousins go, I guess I knew Walter, Marjorie, and Arlen the best because they lived close by. When Walter was 12 and Arlen about six, they were hunting gophers in a culvert, and Walter accidentally shot and killed Arlen. Walter was never the same afterward – so rebellious and hard to handle all his life.

Mom and Dad were both huge influences in my life. Dad, being very particular about what we did, was the disciplinarian in our family. Mom would always say, "You just wait until your Dad gets home!" We would be rewarded by a spank on the bottom. I'm sure I was an ordinary child who did many naughty things. I don't remember anything specific,

The Years Come and Go

but if we got caught doing what we ought not to be doing, we were spanked. Mom was always thinking of her family – the goodies we liked and gifts at birthdays, Christmases, graduations, etc. Money was tight and she squeezed special purchases out of her egg money......whatever she could get for her eggs. Both Mom and Dad were wonderful people. We celebrated their 50th wedding anniversary......it was a very good day. A few months later, Dad died.

We always had company. In those days, people didn't have to call to arrange a visit; they just dropped by on Sunday afternoons and evenings. The kids would play while the grown-ups talked. A lot of Whist and Rummy were played during those visits. I remember that there would be parties, and prizes would be given to high scorers and booby prizes to the lowest ones.

My elementary school days took place in our little one-room school houses.......District #80 in Pencer the first four and a half years and District #112 the last years of elementary school (through grade eight). The enrollment was usually very small, so all the students were friends. Some of my school friends were Leona Moore; Helen, Evelyn, Marie Ann, Elmer, Clifford, Norman, and Marvin Karlstad; Memorie Nelson; Mary Jane Dybedahl; Marjorie and Walter Franklin; and Roy Pearson. Most of the time, we walked to school. When the weather was cold or stormy, however, Dad and the neighbors would take turns driving us in a caboose (a little "house" on a sleigh with a small stove, drawn by a couple of horses). This was sort of a "first bus." We played outdoors at recess. We had little areas in the woods that we used as our playhouse, and in the winter, we skated with shoes on the frozen pond. The teachers were the custodians. I liked all my teachers, but one I especially liked was Rose Evans. I don't know if she was a good or bad teacher, but she was so pretty. She gave each of us a picture at Christmastime, which I cherished for years. I also remember Florence Lind-Janicke, mostly because she slapped my fingers with a ruler and I couldn't remember what I had done.

My first job was working for people named Herling when I was 12 years old. I did odd jobs such as dishes, peeling potatoes and sweeping the floor. I was paid $2.50 a week. The first two years of high school, during the summer, I worked for Mr. and Mrs. Snow. She was a lovely lady; he was a dragon. Their house was crawling with cockroaches – I still get the creeps when I think of them.

I went to Roseau High School. When Norma and I were in high school we had to "board out." We stayed at Ed Johnston's where we had a room. Usually Dad or Mom came to get us for the weekend. During the winter, snow blocked roads or cars wouldn't start due to the cold, so we didn't get home very often. One Saturday morning, Norma and I bundled up and walked home – 21 miles! We hitched a couple of rides for short distances, but we walked for the most part. I don't remember how long it took us but we were home in time to help with some of the chores. I was pretty homesick many times during those years.

The first day I went to high school I got lost – never had been to such a big place. I finally found the door to the outside and ran back to my room where I stayed and cried. I wanted to go home and forget about high school, but I went back the next morning and have never regretted that decision. My biggest problem was being too shy and bashful. It wasn't until my junior and senior years that I dared to "breathe"………during those two years I had such fun and made many friends. I was still scared to death to talk to boys, however. I also remember how scared I felt when Pearl Harbor was bombed. The thought of war was very sobering for me and my friends.

When I was in high school, Roseau's colors were green and white, and they remain the colors today. My favorite movie stars during that time were Clark Gable (so handsome) and Judy Garland (wonderful singer)……also Abbott and Costello. We had an enthusiastic cheerleading squad, which I liked. My favorite cheerleader was Claude Cassidy. One cheer

I can remember: Blood and thunder, brick and tar; Roseau High School, here we are! I graduated from high school in 1942 when I was 17 years old.

After high school, I went to a local teachers' training for nine months. This training prepared us to teach school on a limited certificate. Many years later, the certificate wasn't sufficient, so I took correspondent courses and gained online credits from the University of North Dakota. Later I finished my college career at Bemidji State College…….such a beautiful campus. My major was Elementary Education and my minor was Physical Education, an unusual emphasis at the time, but I think I chose that because the field was quite open and I liked kids.

I taught for close to 40 years and felt very successful as a teacher. I missed teaching so badly when I retired. The summer after my retirement, Gayle asked me to come over to her house for birthday cake and coffee. When I arrived, all my teaching friends were there and we had a little retirement party. Everyone had parked over at Alfred's so I was totally surprised. My friends who were at the party included Shelia Olson, Charlie Klotz, Lorraine Hedlund, Pearl Mitterling, Karen Granitz, and Russel Mitterling.

My first car was an old Model A that I bought from Aunt Ruth when I started teaching school. It wasn't the newest in fashion, but it got me where I wanted to go. I remember thinking that I was pretty hot stuff!

Roy and I went to the same school in grades five to eight. He was a real bully to the little kids and I would chase him with a big stick. We would walk home from school together for the first mile. We were always at odds with each other. I don't remember a first date; I guess we just kind of drifted together. He was a very good-looking man, and one of the things I liked best about him was that he never cursed, swore or told nasty stories. I liked the way his hair fell into a soft wave – he was so neat. But he was very possessive and it was hard to get him to go anywhere special. One day I took the bus to Baudette to visit Norma and Irene. He drove to Baudette to take me home and said, "Either you're going to marry me or else forget it." He was not happy that I had left.

We were married on June 28, 1945, in the Pine Grove Lutheran Church, about seven miles from home. We were the first couple to be married in that new church. It had just been moved from its original site. I thought it was a lovely wedding. Mom and Dad gave us a delicious reception with almost 200 guests. I wore a pretty organza white dress with a train and veil. I thought it was beautiful and had hoped that one of my daughters could wear it someday. I think that Gayle could have worn it but by then it was quite soiled and the material couldn't have withstood a cleaning. Norma and Irene were my attendants. Reverend T. Hanson performed the ceremony. We didn't have a honeymoon right away, and a little later we spent a couple of days in Duluth.

We lived with Grandma and Grandpa Pearson the first year we were married. Then we moved into a little one-room cabin on our land; it was very small but cozy.....I was so happy there. I was an elementary teacher at the time we were married. I was teaching in a one-room school, District 36W. I can't remember the enrollment – about 15 to 20, I think. We surely had a lot of fun.

If I could change one thing about Roy it would be to be more sociable. The first few years he would go with us as a family for some occasions, but as the years went by, those occasions became fewer and fewer. The most serious challenges we faced during the early years of our marriage all had to do with making ends meet, although we lived very frugally. But those were also our happiest years.

After Roy and I were married, we had some good times picking blueberries with Mom and Dad and the kids. I remember one time we found lovely blueberries between some hills and gullies. When it was time to go, we felt disoriented and uncertain about the direction of our car. I panicked, but

Roy kept his head, and we emerged from the forest a long way from the car, knowing where we needed to go.

During some of the long days I spent in our little house while Roy worked in the woods, I would go over to Mom's to listen to her play the piano. She began playing the organ when she was a young girl and became the organist in her church. After she married, she became the pianist and organist at Pine Grove Lutheran Church and continued there until she was 93 years old. It didn't matter that she couldn't see the notes because she played by ear (never had a lesson). Singers requested that she accompany them, and Mom was always eager to oblige. On any given day, she would gather us around the piano at home and we would sing her favorite hymns. Phyllis, Inez, Millie, Freddie, and Sharon had beautiful voices.......the rest of us were average, I guess. I always loved to hear Mom play.

Childhood memories....I have so many of them. I'll start with Christmas. As a child, I was in many Christmas pageants. Mom was very particular about getting us to practice at the church. I remember one Christmas in particular. Dad put hay in a wagon and we were wrapped up in blankets for warmth and off we went to the program. I can't remember why we didn't use the car....probably because there was too much snow or it was extremely cold. What I do remember was that I liked the hay ride to the church.

Dad always went to the woods to get the Christmas tree, usually about one week before Christmas. Most of the time, he would set it up on Christmas Eve or maybe a couple of days before. Each year we'd try to add one or two new decorations to the old collection. All of us kids would string popcorn and cranberries and make little things from paper.

Instead of hanging stockings, Mom and Dad would put presents under the tree on Christmas Eve after we'd all gone to bed. We each got one gift, which was usually something that we needed or wanted badly. Money was very short and both Mom and Dad were so busy taking care of us that they didn't have the time or the energy to make things. Mom was always gracious and appreciated all gifts, big or small. One Christmas all of us kids gave Dad a new gun…..he was always hunting with a very old gun. It was one time when I saw tears in his eyes; it was a very emotional experience.

I don't remember many experiences with Santa (except for being glad that he came every year), but one Christmas, when I wasn't very old, Santa came to our house and wanted to give me a kiss. I hit for the bedroom and slid under the bed to the farthest wall – no way was I going to kiss that whiskered face!

The Holiday Season was a time to be with relatives and friends. This included going to visit Uncle Rudolph who always served potato sausage. We loved having a big meal at

"Auntie" Grace's house, and, of course, there was always a special meal for all the relatives at Mom and Dad's. I loved our Christmas service at church.

My life in our first place holds many impressionable memories for me. I remember running back and forth from the house to outdoor buildings, exchanging German phrases with Mom and Dad. I was not very old, but this memory is very clear in my mind.

We didn't have a very big house – no rugs or linoleum, but Mom scrubbed those floors so that they were squeaky clean (no round corners either!). I can still see and smell the fresh-baked bread sitting on the long kitchen table……and how we'd wait for the butter to be churned so we could eat heaps of mashed potatoes with fresh buttermilk!

My memories of life at our first house make me smile. I remember jumping from the barn roof into the hay beside it….I can still feel the warm sun and smell the hay. I remember skating with our boots on an ice patch that always formed south of the house in the spring. I remember running barefoot all the time in the summer, feeling the mud between my toes and making lovely mud pies, not caring enough about the possibility of stubbed toes, stickers in the field, and the puncture wounds caused by stepping on nails to put on shoes. By the way, measles, mumps, and chicken pox were common childhood illnesses. In fact, if one of the above was going around the neighborhood, we were given direct contact so we would get it too and "be done with it," as Mom would say. She believed that those diseases were easier on children than on adults, so we tried to have them all when we were young. On a less positive side, we had no running water so it was the outhouse which seemed to be always calling us at night when no one wanted to go and didn't want to accompany someone who needed to go.

When we were sick – or to prevent sickness – Mom prepared various home remedies to take the place of store-bought medicines. One of those remedies was a delicious cough syrup from onions. I don't remember all the ingredients, but the main one was onions. Each spring, after the long winter, we would get a dose of sulphur and molasses – to "clean up the blood." And something else that worked for us were poultices made from flax or cream and flour to draw out infections.

I remember the fun we had herding cows because it seemed that the cows were always good……it wasn't something that we wanted to do every day but, as young as we were, we knew that it had to be done. The pastures were seriously dry and the crops were very poor during the drought of the 30s. Then, after the drought the rains came and wouldn't quit, so farmers had to put skids under their swathers in order to harvest. It was hard to stay cool on the hottest days – no electricity so no fans or air conditioners. We stripped as much as possible, made paper fans which helped some, but our arms became tired of fanning. Heat during the haying season was the worst. I never liked the big zigzag lightning or the cracking thunder when I was small, but at least the storms would break the heat streak for a short time anyway.

I remember listening for the whippoorwill at 10:00 every night and walking to the garden north of the house. I remember the animals we always had around us: turkeys that laid their eggs in the brush or in little huts that Dad constructed for them; mother hens coming out of the woods with many little yellow puff balls following them, clucking and peeping; geese that chased us when we went to the toilet……..I loved all of them. Dad would catch baby rabbits while working in the fields and bring them home. They were so cute! Spring meant babies – baby chicks, baby turkeys, goslings, calves, colts, and lambs. I had a wonderful – some would say, magical – childhood!

One of my favorite memories was climbing trees. By our house, there were some big pine trees and Walter and I would see how high we dared to go. One time my foot slipped and I fell, catching my upper arm on a dry branch. The result was a nasty gash – vessels, muscles and everything sticking out. I still have the scar today. Doctors were a luxury in those days, so Mom and Dad had to use the medicines and remedies they had on hand. My injury was pretty bad and most likely would have required many stitches if I had gone to the doctor, but Mom was faithful in treating that wound every day. It healed fine and I didn't mind the scar.

I can remember, as a very young child, Dad putting hay in the wagon so that we could go to the Christmas program at church. It was cold (seems like the winters were all long and cold; we just naturally accepted the fact!), and Mom laid quilts and a buffalo robe on the hay and we all crawled in. We were all "dolled up" but how we looked when we got to church, I don't remember. I've often wondered if Dad got cold driving the horses. As there got to be more of us kids, Dad stopped going to church, but Mom continued to be faithful in getting us all ready to go......not only on Sundays but during the week to practice for Luther League programs, socials, and such. She learned to drive the old Model A and, in some way or other, we got to have a social life, regardless of the weather. She was a wonderful mother.

The Saturday before Easter Sunday we took our baths, washed our hair, and got ready for Easter for that was a very important day for our family. When we were small, Mom colored the eggs after we had gone to bed. She made rabbit nests of hay or straw outside on the south side of the house. Even though money was scarce she always managed a treat from the Easter Bunny, along with the eggs. After we got older, we helped color the eggs – dozens and dozens of them! Everyone got two eggs – one plain one and one with our name on it. After Easter Sunday dinner, Dad was the Easter Bunny and hid the eggs – what fun we had! Roy has carried on that tradition in our family today, and I like that.

I don't remember the bad things: the mosquitos; whether we children were clean or dirty; the fighting which I'm sure we did; the heat; the work......I was happy. I know that Mom and Dad worked very hard but I don't remember them ever complaining. As I reminisce, it seems that we put so much emphasis today on keeping everything, including the children, squeaky clean and up to date. But those are not the values that made an impression on me as a child. I've forgotten many details, but I do remember that I was happy. Mom and Dad were not wealthy so we didn't have many extras, but that didn't seem to affect my happiness. We all worked and played together. We loved and liked each other......still do today and want to get together as a family as often as possible. God blessed our family greatly.

Then we moved to our new place. The government bought the farms within the area that became the "reserve." The old neighbors all bought new land, built new homes and drifted apart – kind of sad. I don't have such distinct memories of my childhood in our new place because I was older then – about ten, I think. I remember thinking that our new home was wonderful – lots more room with a full basement and upstairs. I remember the chores I did at that time: dishes, helping with the wash, cooking, doing what was necessary to keep the house livable, milking cows by hand, herding cows during drought, shocking bundles of grain, and picking grub. I disliked shocking grain the most because when it had to be done, you did it even if it was hot and sticky outside. There always was the problem of stickers mixed with the grain. I tell you, after a hot, humid day of shocking, you were tired and ready for bed!

The Fourth of July was a special holiday that we celebrated with a picnic, usually at the Warroad Park, unless it was haying weather which meant that we would have to stay home and hay and just go to Warroad for the evening fireworks. We kids usually had some fireworks to set off ourselves – pop guns, firecrackers, sparklers and the more powerful ones that we had to let the adults set off. This is another tradition that has been carried over into our married life; as a family, we still enjoy the Fourth of July picnic and fireworks. When I think about picnics, we didn't always go to a park or somewhere else for one; sometimes we picnicked at home. It was a special occasion for us kids to roast hot dogs and marshmallows over a fire whenever Dad had a pile of wood to burn.

Every year we looked forward to the Roseau County Fair which was a time to see people we hadn't seen all summer and have fun. The fair was a three-day affair, but we got to go only one day and evening. When I was very young, Dad always went with us but, as he grew older, he would stay home and go to bed. We had a certain amount of money for the rides which cost ten cents each. My favorites were the merry-go-round, the Ferris wheel, live horses and the tilt-a-whirl.

I loved to play bingo and go fishing. My Uncle Rudolph was such a lucky Bingo player.......he'd come home with his arms full of prizes, such as blankets, kitchen utensils, and various other items. Sucker fishing on the banks of the rivers in the spring – oh, what fun! We'd bring along a frying pan so that we could have fresh fish fried on the fire that Dad built. Many times Dad rented a boat from someone and we'd go fishing by the blinkers on Lake of the Woods. In those days, fish were plentiful and we'd always catch enough for several meals.

I never needed an imaginary friend while growing up because I had all the companionship I needed from my sisters......besides, I never had the time or money to hang out with friends. I never wanted to be alone either. I've always enjoyed being with people and I still love company or any kind of gathering. I guess that comes from being a part of a large family.

When I was young, I wore my hair straight with bangs (no perms to speak of). Mom, however, was the one who had such a pretty hair style. She used a curling iron, heated in the lamp chimney, to make a couple of waves in the front. Then she teased her hair and made a little "puff ball" over each ear and two in the back. I loved that style, but later on she got a perm.

I also loved to sew when I was young, and it seemed to be a natural thing for me to do. After I got married, I made many of the children's clothes and some of mine for teaching. Now, I spend a lot of time piecing quilt tops and crocheting afghans and little blankets. I've always had this desire to make old things look nice.......I would redo furniture rather than throw it away. I guess I was like my mother in that regard. She loved to do needlework and, in her later years, painted pictures to give away to her family.

A list of my favorite things, both then, and some now, include the following: The loveliness of fall; Baby Ruth and Oh Henry candy bars; divinity and fudge; Mom's fried chicken, corn on the cob, apple and whipped cream salad and glorified rice; the "Lone Ranger," "Mr. Boe's Amateur Hour" and "Ma Perkins" radio shows; family get-togethers, especially in the fall when Uncle Rudolph and Aunt Marie served potato sausages and Mom and Dad turkey and trimmings; math and English (science was my least favorite because it just consisted of another book of readings.....no experiments); infrequent trips to town, especially the Red Owl store which I remember with great fondness; burning leaves; my first watch given to me on graduation day; tipping toilets on Halloween; going dancing with a date on New Year's Eve and feasting at one relative's place or another on New Year's Day; wearing green on St. Patrick's Day and being able to pinch someone who forgot to wear the color; trips to North Dakota to visit relatives.....so many aunts, uncles and cousins; ice cream cones; dances: the Fox Trot, Schottische, Polka and Bunny Hop (never learned how to boogie); songs: "Blueberry Hill" and "Mockingbird Hill"; Bible camp at Wabanica by Baudette with Norma; parades, especially the marching bands and those where my grandchildren participate (Roy and I also went to some parades in Thief River); learning how to ride a bike, probably Margie's or Walter's; and all of the seasons as they change (could never live where the seasons were just a name on the calendar). I should mention also that I love all animals and they seem to know it. When Wayne began his beef herd, I was very happy and, until I got too old, I would spend a lot of time with the cows. Today I have Morris, Toby and Bufie......I do enjoy them so much.

(As I stated at the beginning, this is a journal consisting of questions that Joyce asked Mom to complete. It is only fitting, then, that I end this chapter with her personal note.)

The day you were born, Joyce, it was cold and very stormy. We were at Grandpa and Grandma Clasen's. Dad was working in the woods with his brothers, so Grandpa had to go and get him. You were born at Grandpa and Grandma's – Dr. Berge came out and delivered you. I was never so glad to see anyone! Grandma took very good care of us and when it was time to go home after a couple of weeks, Grandpa said, "Are you sure you should go? Stay a little longer." He evidently didn't mind having us there.

You were a very pretty baby – olive skin and dark hair with a little curl at the end. You had the most beautiful braids, thick and rich-looking. You were vivacious and so very neat...... Judy, being the opposite, drove you crazy! You liked to sew and make little things in the old Singer machine. Gayle loved your little pouches with zippers. By the way, Judy stayed with Uncle Raymond and Aunt Myrtle when you were born because she had the chicken pox and I didn't want you to get it.

And now, Sissy, I've forgotten so many of the details of your growing up days. It seems all I can remember are good things. The bad was there, I'm sure, but it certainly wasn't a main ingredient in my life. I've even forgotten much of what happened when you kids were growing up. But I do remember how much I loved you (and all of you kids) and tried to give you the important things. Hopefully, you remember the greater part of your life as being good. Now, in my later years, a lot of my activities are still concerned with you. You have given Dad and me so much; the gift of yourself has always filled our hearts with thanksgiving. The best gift I can give you is my prayer that your faith in God and Jesus Christ will grow and remain firm. Have faith and trust in Him at all times. Be kind and good to those around you. Then we will all be together in that big circle in Heaven, forever and forever.

Chapter 7

2000 – 2002

(2000, 2001, and 2002 calendar summaries)

A new commandment I give to you, that you love one another; just as I have loved you; you also are to love one another. By this all people will know that you are my disciples, if you have love for one another.

John 13: 34-35

2000 Calendar Summary

January began on a frigid note (0-20 below) and continued to be a cold month. Temperatures varied from 30 degrees with the sun shining and no wind to 10 to 15 degrees above zero with some snow to minus 30 degrees and an extremely cold wind. Katie and Josh paid a surprise visit home and managed to arrange a fishing trip which produced five small fish and a lot of warm coziness. Mom's amaryllis bloomed on January 22nd; the water froze on January 27th; and Mom went fishing on the 29th.

The Years Come and Go

Except for the second week, February appeared to have been a relatively mild month with temperatures hovering around 20 to 40 degrees…….above zero! Mom fertilized her plants on the first of the month and dried clothes on the line the third week. She commented that the snow and ice were melting every day. Jon came on the 26th and on the 27th, everyone was "out west," a comment that I didn't understand at first, but then realized she was talking about the family ski trip to Tahoe. Jon and Rozie stayed home on the farm.

Mom announced that spring had arrived with the beautiful weather marked by 60-degree temperatures the first week of March. Then, on March 8th, temperatures plunged to six degrees and remained very cold for another week. Katie turned 21 while many of us were skiing in Tahoe. Nice weather returned to close out the last two weeks in March. Ten calves were born during the warm weather; unfortunately, one cow died. Mom and Dad went to Hoyt Lakes to visit Gerry and Don; Wayne purchased a "new" car; and the robins made their debut on the farm.

The only weather comments for the month of April were made regarding the first two weeks when temperatures hovered around 15 degrees with a cold rain most of the day on April 2nd. I spent a week on the farm in the middle of the month, and Dan (Lisell?) appeared to be building something since his name appeared on the calendar frequently during the last two weeks. Eight calves were born in April, followed by three more in May. Mom's only comment on the weather for May appeared on the third week: "two good weeks – few showers."

The cattle were in the draw on June 1st; the bulls were out on the 9th; everyone was together in the east pasture on the 24th; and all were up north at the end of the month. The first part of June was marked by rainy and chilly weather (50 degrees). Heavy rains (three and a half to four inches) descended on June 13th and beautiful days followed to finish the month. Wayne baled 22 bales of hay.

Mom noted that Jenny came home on the first of July and all the kids went to Toledo. The 2000 calendar was the Omaha Home for Boys Calendar. Mom contributed to this charity, and the calendar was given to her in appreciation for her generosity.

2001 Calendar Summary

(Note at the top of the calendar: In January – Children's Mission, Omaha Home, Wilkerson. I believe that those are the charities Mom chose for her contributions that month.)

January appeared to be a fishing month. Hannah and

Tony went fishing on January 2nd; they each caught eight fish. Then, Dad and Tony had very good luck on the 12th, but the men had no luck on the 20th. The first two weeks and the last week of the month featured mild weather with no snow; the third and fourth weeks were cold and windy with lots of sun (0 to 15 below). Dad and Mom went to Thief River three times that month. A little calf died and another was born. A cow got in with the bull, and Mom wonders if she was bred. Two more calves were born in February when it was quite blustery and cold (minus 15 degrees). The cold continued throughout the month (got down to 20 below). Mom enjoyed a good Bible study at Inez's on February 4th and attended Vivian Olson's funeral on the 7th (97 years old). Linsay and Matt ended their visit on the 5th; Hannah stayed home from school on the 6th, the same day that Wayne left for North Dakota. Mom made an appointment with Dr. Herseth and fertilized her plants on the 17th. Everyone left for skiing at Boyne on February 15th and returned on the 20th.

March came in like a lamb with a temperature of 40 degrees and sunny skies….. Mom hung clothes on the clothesline. The month quickly took the shape of a lion, however, with five degrees to ten degrees below zero. From that point on, the temperatures vacillated so that one day it was warm and the next cold. Katie celebrated her birthday on March 4th, and Wayne and his friend, Greg, embarked on a camping trip the next weekend when one day it was ten degrees below zero and the next 35 degrees above zero! Ten calves were born during the month and a cow died; Mom mentioned that No. 9 was alive (she was happy about that!). Linsay and Matt visited for four days, and I visited for a week. The month ended on a warm note: 46 degrees with Mom hanging clothes on the line again, as she did at the beginning of the month. She fertilized her plants and had her hair done.

Seven calves were born in April on mostly beautiful spring days. It was 46 degrees and snowing on April 1st, and for the next few days, it was cold, rainy and snowy, but it got better after that with temperatures in the 50s, 60s, 70s (and one day with 80 degrees). Rod fixed the stove; Mom visited Grandma, washed clothes which she hung on the line, and fertilized her plants; Dad worked with the banking on the house; and Mom attended a Mother-Daughter banquet at the Roseau Covenant Church with Gayle which she said was a lot of fun. Thunder showers marked the end of April and the beginning of May, a month that Mom described as beautiful weather with lovely rain showers and an occasional thunder storm until……..it snowed on May 22nd! A little calf was born, probably in the south pasture where the cows and bulls were gathered. Phyllis and Gerry came up to see Grandma on May 11th.

The month of June brought an abundance of rain, a little

sun, and 90 - degree temperatures. The cows moved around to their usual habitats, and one cow became sick. The "kids" spent a weekend in Minneapolis. Mandy's shower took place on the 23rd, and on June 30th, she and Chris were married. I arrived at the farm on the 28th and then Mom and Dad went to Boyne with me on July 2nd. Grandma Rosie died on July 8th, while Mom was on her way home. Grandma's funeral was on July 12th, the day before Mom's birthday.....it was a beautiful day. The weather was very hot and humid in the middle of the month (85 – 90 degrees) and rainy at the end. Wayne went to Iowa for a couple of days. Two calves and one cow were treated twice for foot rot.

The weather words for the first part of August were "hot, hot, and hot." The heat moderated during the last two weeks so that, while the days were hot, there was no humidity and the nights were cool. On August 16th, the church women went to Susan's, and Mom and Dad visited Gerry and Don the next day. On August 18th, Jackie was married. On one of those extremely hot days, Joyce took Hannah and Jena for a long ride to Duluth in Bill's air-conditioned van. The heat continued for the first couple of weeks in September (90 degrees), except for September 13th when it froze (27 degrees)! The third and fourth weeks showcased beautiful fall weather, and during that time, Mom and Dad went to Duluth and enjoyed the church picnic at the Penturan Church on the Ridge. Linsay and Matt came home for a visit the first weekend. On September 9th, the World Trade Towers in New York City collapsed.

Mom and Dad spent a week with us in Toledo in October. During their time away, the weather was beautiful, despite a killer frost on October 6th (19 degrees). Two days after their return, a winter storm hit.......it delivered four inches of wet snow and a beastly north wind. The last few days of the month were dreary and cold, but no rain or snow. Millie hosted the Bible study on October 7th.

Opening deer hunting weekend was gorgeous and productive: Chris shot one deer; Willie three; and Wayne and Hannah got one together. Indian Summer turned into cooler days but they were still beautiful. Jack celebrated his birthday at the Jakt Stuga on November 11th, the second week of deer hunting. Linsay, Matt and Katie joined him the following weekend and they all went home on the 23rd. Dad mowed the grass at Ed's two days before it snowed two inches. Mom, Gayle, Joyce and Pam met me in Minneapolis on November 30th for the women's weekend.

December was a busy month. Mom had her hair done right before she went to Minneapolis, and she was ready for Christmas. It was a relatively mild month, especially at the beginning with 25-degree highs and eight-degree lows. It rained on the 15th and then it snowed, but the sun melted it. Christmas week was cold (minus eight and 12 degrees) and that temperature stayed through New Year's Eve. A little calf was born on the 8th, and several calves were sold for a good price. Linsay and family came home on the 22nd; and Jenny and family and Katie arrived on the 23rd. They all left the weekend of the 29th. Mom was happy to report that a family get-together after Christmas was attended by 32 members.

2002 Calendar Summary

January temperatures ranged from eight degrees below zero to 40 degrees above zero……it was beautiful weather, Mom said. During the week of January 7th, when the temperatures reached highs of 40, 38, and 28 degrees, Mom enthused about the sunshine and blue skies. She washed clothes one day and helped clean the 11 fish that the guys caught one weekend (Tony caught "a big one"). She also attended Bible study at Yvonne's, went with Gayle to Baudette and to Thief River, and visited Rose Mitterling in Grand Forks with Dad one day. On January 27th, the family gathered for a fish fry and planned to go snocatting but it turned out to be too cold. Linsay and Jack had an accident in Duluth on January 29th. It turned colder with snow flurries at the end of the month. Mom commented on the off-heat being off for "the first time this season."

It was sunny and 20 below on February 1st. The men went fishing when it warmed up to five degrees above. Linsay, Matt and Jack came home for a few days. Phyllis and Mark's visit the second week initiated a lot of socializing with the Clasens.......Mom and Dad had Inez, Bill, Phyllis and Oliver over for supper one night, and hosted a "wonderful day with family." At Joyce's birthday party on February 10th, people went snocatting. Mom and Dad snocatted to Colin's cabin the next day. Mom noted that Wayne left for camp. On February 14th, Joyce and Rod and Pam and Wayne made their annual ski trek to Boyne. Temperatures moderated the last week of the month so that Mom washed clothes and dried them outside on a day when it was 41 degrees! A week later, it was 12 below and the water froze. Rozie had her last game and Hannah her last meet the weekend of the 23rd. Wayne went to Minneapolis on the 26th.........bought a hundred pounds of feed before he left.

Nine little calves were born during the month of March, which began on a cold note (20 below) but warmed up, for the most part. Sunny days and eight inches of fresh snow made for beautiful snocatting to Bemis Hill and its environs. I came home on the 9th and stayed for more than a week. Cy and Eva visited on the 19th; Elaine C. died on the 21st; and Rose's funeral was held on the 28th. Four more calves were born (one to Mulehead) in April, a month which began with snow flurries on several cold days (18 – 25 degrees) and warmed up to a sunny, windy 77-degree day on the 16th! Most of the remainder of the month was relatively cold (20 to 35 degrees) with a strong north wind and a little snow on several days. On April 30th, it was 50 to 60 degrees with no wind. During this month, Mom had an eye appointment, hosted Bible study, and celebrated Seth's birthday.

On the first day of the lovely month of May, it was 30 degrees and snowing, and, until the 11th, it froze almost every night! Mom and Dad planted the garden on May 14th when it was 70 degrees. The next few days were very nice, but the nights produced hard frost, and fierce south and north winds prevailed with a mixture of snow and rain. Linsay was married on May 25th……..a beautiful day with the whole Pearson clan present. Temperatures soared to the 80s during the last week of the month, producing five inches of rain. Mom washed four loads of clothes. The cows and bull resided in the south pasture where a little calf was born.

Fishing was good on June 1st when Dad, Wayne, and Bill caught 18 very nice fish. It rained pretty steadily in June …..a total of around ten inches, with a little hail mixed in on the 14th. Homes for the peripatetic cows were the east pasture, out south, and back to the east pasture where they stayed for a while. Mom said that a new bag of egg maker was started on June 11th. The air conditioner was installed on June 29th when it was 95 degrees. It cooled off for the first part of July and then became hot again. It hailed in Salol and Warroad, while the thunder and lightning produced very little rain on the farm. July must have been a relatively dry month because Mom thanked God for the "perfect shower" when it rained during the last couple of days. Joyce and Rod hosted a picnic at their house. Jon and I were on the farm for two weeks and took the girls to Boyne with us. We picked some blueberries but they were pretty scarce. Mom had her hair done on July 30th.

August was a lovely month......cool with just the right amount of rain. A little calf was born on the 2nd. Mom and Dad went to Boyne (no mention of who went with them) to pick up the girls on August 7th. Imo, Byron and Nikki visited during the beautiful week of August 11th. Joyce and Gayle and their families went to South Dakota on the 21st and returned on the 26th. Mom had a message on the 23rd, the same day she recorded that her blood pressure was lower. The cattle were southwest, east and southeast. A little calf was born at the beginning of the month.

The cattle were on Mom's mind almost all the time, it seems. She was always interested in where they were and how they were doing (e.g., they were offered a new bag of mash on

September first). In September, she recorded, as usual, their grazing pastures: east, southeast, and west. Jack visited on the 5th when it was a humid 85 degrees and climbing, eventually hitting 92 for a couple of days. The rest of the month stayed cool and sunny. Dad and Wayne started repairing the grainery on September 6th; two weeks later, Wayne and the guys started building a road to the camp. Mom made cranberry jelly, which she said turned out to be good. She and Dad went to the Penturen Church, after which they helped Jena celebrate her birthday. The next weekend they enjoyed a visit with Evie, Brandon, Paul, Peggy and Irene.

The first real hard frost occurred on October 4th, and the next week presented a surprise high of 63 degrees, followed by colder than normal temperatures (highs in the 40s and lows in the 20s and 30s). During the warm spell, Mom washed clothes and dried them outside. It got colder as the month progressed until the 31st when it was 10 degrees. Mom and Dad left for Toledo on the 17th and returned on the 28th. While they were away, Wayne fed the cattle and must have shingled the grainery. Snow covered the ground on October 29th.

Opening deer season weekend yielded five deer in weather that was mostly cold and dreary (30 degrees to five below). Three inches of snow fell on November 12th, and for the rest of the month temperatures ranged from 25 degrees above zero to five below zero. Wayne sold calves; Mom bought 100 pounds of chicken feed and hung clothes out on the line; and Jack celebrated his birthday on one of the beautiful, sunny November days.

It was a white Christmas, probably the first Christmas held at Pam and Wayne's. Mom said, "It was a wonderful Christmas season. Our family collected nearly $1000 to give to Salem Church and Teen Challenge." Dad and Mom bought a pool table for the Jakt Stuga. An eight-foot Christmas tree presided in their living room. Bill, Zach, Jon and I arrived at the farm at 2:00 a.m. on December 26th. Dad had successful surgery at the beginning of the month, and the girls – but not Mom this year – made their annual trek to meet me in Minneapolis. According to Mom's notes, temperatures remained fairly moderate throughout the month (28 above to a couple of days of five below) and just the right amount of snow fell……..a sweet ending to 2002.

Chapter 8
From the "Wild Flowers of North America" journal

2001 – January, 2002

(This is Mom's most comprehensive and detailed journal writing.)

In peace, I will lie down and sleep, for you alone, O Lord, will keep me safe.
Psalm 4:8

I will never fail you. I will never abandon you.
Hebrews 13:5

2001 Journal Entries
January – Week 1

It's a very cold and quiet New Year's Day. All our company

has left. Pam and Joyce took down our Christmas tree......so sad to throw it away.

The rest of the week included a trip to Thief River where Roy had his eyes checked and we bought groceries. We also went to Warroad twice, once with our checks (supposed to get an increase), and again so that Roy could get the Jag fixed and buy a tire for the car. Both days were cloudy and mild. A baby calf was born, but he froze to death. I always feel so bad when that happens.

I woke up at five o'clock one morning and realized that early risings were getting to be the norm, rather than the exception. Then, one day I slept in late and had a wonderful day. Joyce and family came out after church, and we all visited with Gayle, Bill and Wayne. Judy called to wish us a Happy New Year. Oh, how I praise God for His wonderful, precious promises and for His care. He leads me every day.....my hand in His. Truly, my cup runneth over.

February - Week 2

The weather is so nice, day after day – some wind and cold but the winter, for the most part, has been very enjoyable. Linsay and Matt were here for a visit, and Tony left for his job. I found out that Hannah's arm will be okay, but she had a bad night – fever and headache – when she and Buford stayed with us and she slept until noon. She is such a little sweetheart.

Now the weather has turned colder (15 degrees and 30 below a couple of nights), and the water froze, but it didn't take the guys long to thaw it out. Tony came home one afternoon and he, Roy and Kevin went fishing; they caught five fish. I went with Gayle to the Northwest Angle. Vivian Olson died (97 years old) and I went to her funeral on a very cold day. I pray that Vivian had accepted God's grace and so is at peace with Him.

On a quiet, clear morning, Roy was hurt by a cow with a calf, trying to get them into the barn. The mother was just trying to protect her calf whom she thought was at risk of being hurt, but it was still a bad thing for Roy. The rest of the week was marked by another fishing trip which yielded only a couple of fish and a celebration of Joyce's birthday. Wayne and Pam went to a hockey game one night and picked up Rozie……Hannah and Buford were once again overnight guests. Judy is at Boyne.

Week 3

It's a very quiet and cold day (20 degrees) – a good day that the Lord has made so we will rejoice and be glad in it…..and praise Him mightily! Chad picked up the cow and calf that hurt Roy; Wayne is very relieved. I went to Bible study and visited with Mom who was not feeling so hot. While there, I learned that Vivian is in the hospital for congestion; she has lost so much weight. Roy and I also went to Warroad one day to visit Margaret Lindholm…..we had a great visit.

It remains cold but nice. Everyone has left for Boyne. Roy made lopschoush and it was very good, as usual. I got a pink rose from my Secret Pal…..so lovely and uplifting. Judy called and told us that Jon was crowned king of his class.

We had communion on Sunday. Jesus did so much for me and I wish that I could do something good for Him. Shawn, Kevin, Sharon and Seth came out for a while. We had a good visit, especially with Seth while Roy and Kevin talked. After they left, we went to have a piece of birthday cake with Freddy who is 64 today. We also visited Vivian.

Week 4

The gang came home today. Everyone had a good time skiing and being together…….thank you, God! It's a cold day (30 degrees below zero)…..the water froze and we had no Bible study. Mom's sinuses are bad, but she says that she's feeling better. Hannah visited us after school. Wayne left for Minneapolis and will be there for a few days.

It's been warming up throughout the week. One morning it was five below and another it was 20 above. It snowed one night so everything looked so white and clean the next morning. That's the way it is with our ugly, dirty sins covered by the blood of Jesus; they are truly washed away. Roy, Tony and I went fishing….Tony caught seven and Roy had a few bites. I was just glad to be along because it's so cozy in the fishing shack.

We went to Shelley's reception where Mom looked so pretty and was feeling a lot better. But Gayle got sick and had to delay her departure for Minneapolis where she was supposed to be for meetings.

It stormed at the end of the week, so we didn't go to church. Roy and I fried fish for supper, and it tasted so good.

March – Week 1

March 1st came in like a lamb……40 degrees with sunshine, and the snow is packing and settling. I went with Roy to Thief River for groceries and the usual Arctic Cat inspection. It was a good day until Roy's nerves got bad and he called me a name I didn't deserve. I felt so low, but it was such a beautiful day and things got better for Roy. Praise God for His love!

I finished the Kincaid puzzle, and that, in itself, bolstered my spirits; it's such a lovely scene. Tony came home from Bemidji where he was promoted to supervisor on his job. The guys all went to take the fish house off the lake. What a beautiful day for that task!

Pam and Wayne went to the Winter Home Show in Grand Forks on a day that was colder than it had been (five degrees below). It's Katie's birthday......I pray that she's having a great day.

Week 2

The sun is shining but it is chilly (five degrees below). A little calf was born and is doing well......praise God for that! We went to Warroad where we cashed our checks, had dinner with Wayne, and visited Vivian who looks and feels much better. We also went to Warroad another day for lunch with the kids. It's fun to get out of the house and socialize with people you like.

We had two Bible studies this week: a study on Proverbs at Yvonne's with five ladies present and one at our house with Inez, Millie, Annette, Gayle, Pam and Roy present. I pray that God was glorified at both Bible studies and everyone received a blessing.

Russel Dahl died and his funeral was on Saturday. Thanks to you, oh God, for your salvation. Kevin fixed our ceiling, so now that is done. Wayne went camping with Greg; I fear they'll catch their death of cold!

A long day……no company. The good news is that Wayne is back and he didn't freeze to death!

Week 3

Judy came home for a visit, and the weather was perfect while she was here…..glorious days of snocatting with Roy and Wayne and Pam after work. We did a lot of gallivanting – to see Helen and have lunch with Inez and Bill, Annette, and Millie and Robert in Roseau; to say goodbye to Grandma Rosie (Judy) who was feeling chipper and very talkative; to watch Jenny play basketball in Grygla; and to have supper with everyone in Warroad (with a side trip to the casino where we had no luck at all).

I made a corn beef dinner for whoever came over and a banana cream pie, mostly for Roy. It was a lazy day. We found out that Linsay and Matt are engaged. We went to the Malung Carnival in the evening…..always fun to meet people and participate in the cake walk.

We had a delicious breakfast at Gayle and Bill's and then

went to church. We had to leave early to take Judy to the airport. It was so good to have her home. She had an uneventful flight home and I praise God for watching over her.

Week 4

The days are cloudy with temperatures above freezing (one day it was 47 degrees!) and melting snow. The sun comes out periodically and it's lovely when it does. Wayne lost a cow and doesn't know the reason. Gayle received the good news that she got 95% on her test. Eva and Mary stopped in for a visit; it was a wonderful surprise, and we had a good time together. We had Bible study and then visited with Mom for a while.

The sun is shining but it's very cold…..0 degrees at six o'clock this morning. It snowed a little so everything looks clean, but I'm sure the snow will melt shortly. Irene leaves for Louisiana, and Inez, Bill, Millie and Robert are driving to Colorado.

What a cold day – I wonder if it will ever warm up! Did January return? My back hurts badly and my stomach is on the blink. Tomorrow will be better. Linsay and Matt came home so we got to see Linsay's beautiful ring. I pray that God will bless them greatly…..who knows what plans He has for them.

I watched a video at church which touched me very much. I felt restless all day.

Week 5

It's Roy's birthday today – 76 years old! Some of the gang brought out an ice cream cake to share…..as always, when we get together, it was a good day. It was five below when the day began but it warmed up…..no terrible north wind. I'm so glad that God is in control of everything, including the weather. What a mess we would make of things if we were in control! I had my hair done at Golden Shears, and it looks like I got a good perm. We visited with Mom while in Roseau and talked to Inez about their trip to Colorado.

Another gloomy morning – 32 degrees at seven o'clock and it's looking like rain. Calves are being born on a regular basis…….such a wonderful sign of the new life of spring. Gayle, Bill and Tony went to Minneapolis to meet Jenny from New York. I'm glad they went and very much at peace that Wayne is around.

April – Week 1

April Fool's and it's snowing! But I'm sure that new life is waiting to lift its head above the ground as soon as it warms up. Roy had another birthday cake.

It did warm up…..almost 50 degrees today. I spent some time outside but mostly just tussled around. I spent quite a bit of time working on an afghan which I think is going to turn out well. Roy fixed the stove, so now I don't have to worry about that. Wayne came home early and Gayle stopped in after work.

How quickly the weather changes! It's been overcast with wet snow for two days. We didn't have Bible study because Yvonne went to Minneapolis, so we went to Warroad to have lunch with Joyce and Rod instead. Roy came with me to visit Mom – how happy she was to see him! Rozie also visited Grandma Rosie. Helen is depressed……I hate to know that my friend feels so low.

Tony and Roz went to Duluth for a couple of days. God provided a safe trip with the foggy conditions. The girls had their annual rummage sale. I didn't go because of the weather – snow, sleet, rain and an "out of control" north wind. Pam and Wayne went to Bemidji to buy a furnace. It's Seth's birthday. I pray God's richest blessings on that little boy. Roy cleaned the carpet for me; he also mopped the porch and cleaned the car. I am grateful.

Week 2

I was sick for about three days, so I slept more than usual. I couldn't go to Bible study and I didn't visit Mom. Wayne and Roy started cutting wood. I woke up one morning to see a lot of water standing around because of all the rain we've had. I wonder if the Red River flooded last night. This thought makes me fret and stew but I must remember that God is in control.

I was finally able to go see Grandma Rosie. When I told her how pretty she looked she said, "Well, it's Easter, you know!" Joyce and family had been in to see her in the morning and Mom was truly happy to see them. We also stopped to see Margie who is doing pretty well.

Saturday was a beautiful day. Shawn and Joyce mopped the floors and cleaned the house for Easter. But then on Sunday, the weather changed and I was tempted to wish everyone a "Merry Christmas!" It's a good thing the weather has nothing to do with how we celebrate Easter. We had about 20 for Easter breakfast and we worshipped and praised the Lord in church afterwards. The Pearson clan practically filled all the pews in the church! Wayne and Pam went to Grand Forks after the egg hunt which had to take place in the Quonset where Roy had hidden the eggs because of the nasty weather. Roy and I had a delicious supper at Gayle's.

Week 3

Mostly cold, dreary weather and still blowing, but the next day it was nice with sunshine, no wind and temperatures in the 50s. Katie, Linsay and Matt went back to school. Roy is working up north with wood and I'm cleaning upstairs …… closets I haven't seen in years. I visited Mom who wasn't feeling well and planned to go to Bible study, but it turns out there wasn't any Bible study so I went to see Inez instead. She is such an inspiration. We prayed for Missy and Oliver.

It's a gorgeous day – no rain and 70 degrees. I spent time outdoors but I couldn't do much because we've had so much rain the water is very high in the yard…….my poor flowers. Tony didn't stop in.

Lots of rain already this morning……first thunderstorms of the season. It cleared in the afternoon and Roy drained the yard so it looks nice. I went to a Mother-Daughter banquet at Gayle's church. We had a good lunch and a nice program; I won a prize for the most innovative hat!

We went to church and then spent the day basically alone. The human spirit is resilient – it knows when the hurt is gone and love and kindness takes its place……but sometimes it takes a long time.

Week 4

What a beautiful, sunny day….76 degrees! We went to Warroad to get trees for Gayle and Bill and had coffee with the Warroad gang. I started to tie a second quilt and washed four loads of clothes which I dried on the line. I spent a lot of time outdoors but it's still too wet to "dig." It's Judy's birthday.

Bible study: always such a blessed time I hate to have it end. It was at Millie's today and I visited Mom afterward, but she wasn't feeling well again. She felt better by the time Inez and I left. I pray that God will take care of her. Wayne redid the flower beds, just before the thunder and lightning hit.

May – Week 1

The month started with thunder showers. Evie, Brandon, Peggy and Irene surprised us with a visit. I went to Bible study and I couldn't help but think of what a privilege it is to have this little group to fellowship with – bless us all, Lord, and bless Yvonne. I saw Mom.......her eyes looked so much better and she sounded better too; she even smiled a little.

It's a great day to be outside. Daffodils are open and their little faces are so lovable! Roy planted potatoes and I put in onions, carrots and beets. Joyce and family were out and Wayne and the guys dug the footings for the addition while the girls washed the windows and did other things around the house.

On this day it's overcast and rainy, but the guys got all the siding of Wayne's house off. I went to see Mom.....she is not good at all. Judy called to tell us that she had a nice birthday party.

Week 2

A beautiful sunny day which should be spent outside but I'm too worried about Mom to enjoy it. After Bible study, I went over to visit her; she's not rallying this time.......does not eat or drink. I keep putting her in God's care.

I feel sad about Linsay, but she and Matt will be fine. God loves them both and if they let Him, He'll lead them all the way. Rozie looked beautiful for her band concert; this is Pladson's last one. They started Mom on an IV.….she seems to be doing a little better but is still not well.

Phyllis, Gerry and Don came to be with Mom. They took the IV out of her and then re-instated it because she can't eat. Should we let her go? What is God's plan for her?

Mother's Day……such beautiful weather! The church service was very inspiring. The kids came and worked for me for my Mother's Day present. Gerry, Don and Phyllis were here in the evening. It was a very good day.

Week 3

The birds are singing so profusely this morning. We have

the windows open so we can really enjoy them. It rained a little last night. We don't have Bible study so I worked hard outside, and now my back really hurts. Wayne is busy hauling fill for his yard.

Phyllis came back to stay with Mom (Gerry stayed)…..it's such a joy to be around her. Mom's x-rays showed no blockage so why can't she eat or drink? It's another beautiful day, so I worked in the flower beds and helped clean the church.

It's a cold, rainy, dreary day. I went to see Mom and was dismayed because she is not doing well at all. Joyce, Jena and Seth came out while I was gone. We all went to Bible study at Gayle's. I came down with a bad cough in the evening.

Week 4

It rained most of the day and then turned to snow which quickly melted. I didn't sleep well last night and I don't feel well today, but I went to see Mom anyway……..had a good little visit but she's so weak. She says she doesn't want to die because she might miss out on a family event! I can't figure it out…..Mom lies there day after day, too weak to even feed herself, and yet she wants to live.

Everyone left for Matt's graduation today. Roy and I went to Cy's 80th birthday party. A heavy May shower last night made for a beautiful, clean day today……sometimes the sun shines and sometimes it's cloudy.

June – Week 1

I spent the entire day with Mom. She had so many visitors that we didn't get much of a chance to reminisce. They inserted an IV and that perked her up. The next day I went to Thief River with Roy. It was a lovely day but I felt that I should have been home. Irene, Evie and Millie are with Mom who is not getting any better. Lord willing, she will soon be free from pain.

It's the last day of school. Hannah received five ribbons in the Malung-A-Thon and a certificate for being a B student throughout the year. There was no rain last night so maybe I'll get most of the lawn done.

It rained hard last night and thunder rolled across the sky. It's so wet I can't work outside. We went to Casey's graduation and saw Mom afterward. She didn't talk at all. Wayne and Pam went to Minneapolis.

Week 1 (again)

Another beautiful day with no rain…..the soil is so saturated that it seems as if it will never dry out, but it will.

Roz and Hannah went to Judy's. Wayne gave diesel fuel to a bloated cow and lifted her up with a loader; she will be okay. Praising the Lord for His goodness and mercy…..

Mom is the same. She says that she's on the road to Heaven. I know that's true but why is it taking so long? We had Bible study in her room. Phyllis and Trish were here to see Mom.

It's a hot, sunny and dry 80-degree day….very good growing day. Bill fixed the water heater. Afterward he, Gayle, Pam, Wayne, Tony and I four-wheeled to Dewey's…...so much fun. We ended the day with supper at Gayle and Bill's.

Week 2

I stayed home most of the day and then went to see Mom in the afternoon. She lies with her eyes shut and doesn't talk but she knows what's going on. It's so sad to see her like that. We had a family picnic in the park in the evening.

It rained a little this morning. We had our last Bible study for the summer. I started another quilt. I went to see Mom for a while. She was so much better – didn't sit up but we had a good conversation. Phyllis's family arrived.

We had a picnic at the Warroad Park with Shawn, Kevin, Chris, Mandy, Wayne and Pam. It was a beautiful day and we had so much fun. The men and Pam went fishing afterward; they caught some nice fish. Phyllis went home.

Week 3

It's a nice day but it rained heavily in the afternoon. I miss "the girls" so much. Mom sounded weak on the phone.

I sat with Mom all afternoon. She was very quiet and answered questions but didn't really converse. Wayne cut the grass at the pond and then we had taco salad with Gayle, Bill, Tony, Wayne and Pam.

Everyone left for Linsay's graduation in Minneapolis. I felt sad that I wasn't with them but knew without a doubt that I should be home. I did go to Mandy's bridal shower the next day. It was 90 degrees with no rain. Afterward, I visited with Mom; she was so quiet but seemed to be at peace. Joyce and Rod were out this evening.

Week 4

Another hot day…..Roy and Raymond went to Thief River. Mom is the same. Jenny, Jesse, Judy, Bill and the boys all arrived for Mandy and Chris's wedding – they had Roz, Hannah and Jena with them.

Chris and Mandy's wedding was so beautiful and a lot

of fun. The day was perfect…not too hot and not too cold. Jon played his violin at the wedding and then at church on Sunday; he also played for Mom. Willie flew back to Columbus. I miss the kids when they leave.

July – Week 1

Roy and I went to Boyne with Judy and her family. It was a long ride but a good one. Thank God for His faithfulness. Jon went back to his camp and Zach to his job at the lumber yard at Boyne. Gayle and Bill joined us at Judy's and we went for a boat ride in the new boat – such a beauty! The river was shallow but the lake was a little rough. The men fished but caught nothing. The ladies went uptown and had lunch at a classy restaurant. We watched a spectacular firework display on the Fourth. Our last day there was leisurely. Roy cut down brush around the deck for Judy and Bill; Tony helped prepare boneless pork chops for a delicious supper on the grill; and we all watched the movie, "The Titans" that evening. The Patberg house at Boyne is so big and can accommodate many people nicely.

We started for home at 9:30 this morning and arrived at 1:30 the next morning – stopped for refreshments along the way. I got a call from Inez: Mom went home to Heaven about midnight. I'm so sad. She leaves a tremendous hole but I'm happy for her. She is home with her God.….no more suffering and sadness for her.

Week 2

We all got together to discuss Mom's funeral and clean out her room. Her "going away party" was well-attended......so many people who laughed and cried. Carson Hedlund sang beautifully and Judy's eulogy was so on track. I miss Mom already.

On my birthday, Inez, Phyllis, Millie, Tootsie, Mark, Sami and Oliver brought out a cake and we looked at Mom's cards......so many of them and memorials totaled $1,397. It rained during the night, which meant no haying so Wayne could join us for a birthday party for Shawn, Sharon and me. We had a good time at the beach. Tony gave us boat rides and the young people went tubing. I fried fish for supper.

Week 3

Fair week and very hot – 85 to 90 degrees all week and a lot of rain. I went to breakfast with six classmates and was surprised to find out that I was the only one with gray hair! We helped Pam and Wayne butcher 20 chickens. Pastor Bill's sermon was so forceful on Sunday. That evening I fried fish for Gayle, Bill, Tony, Chris and Mandy.

Week 4

Wayne spent two days in Iowa and then he and his family went camping at Cass Lake with Pam's family for a couple of days. The weather has changed and it's gorgeous…..so nice and cool. Roy and I went blueberry picking twice during the week……both mornings were beautiful with no heat and no bugs. Inez had surgery on her rupture; everything went well. We treated two calves and one cow for foot rot.

The Warroad people came out on Saturday; they mowed and trimmed the lawn and had blueberry pie. It was another beautiful day. On Sunday, we went to church and then had dinner with Joyce's family. I canned two pints of beans.

August – Week 1

The week began with high winds and about five inches of rain. Poor cattle – so much rain and mud. Water everywhere……Pam and Wayne worked to dry out their basement. Linsay is terribly sick; Hannah came home; and I spent a delightful day at Crazy Daze with Joyce, Sharon, Jena, Seth and Hannah.

Wayne and Pam spent a weekend with Greg and Sally; they enjoyed the concerts despite 100-degree weather. Anton Moser celebrated his 100th birthday at Raygene's house. Joyce, Jena and Hannah went to Judy's…….God, please give them a safe trip. I developed an earache which became progressively worse.

Week 2

My earache was bad last night and so was my shoulder. It is so hot – 90 degrees for three days. The weather turned cool and breezy toward the end of the week. Wayne and Pam left for the East early this morning; Gayle went to Mahnomen and Thief River Falls; Rod flew to Toledo early this morning; and Tony and Bill left for South Dakota to fish for trout. Oh, that God will bless all the trips.

Shawn, Kevin, and Sharon came out to have dinner with us; we had a delightful time. Inez, Millie, Annette, and little Oliver came and we had Bible study on the wonderful Jesus who is our Savior. Ollie and Roy had a great time getting acquainted; they did some four-wheeling. God bless and care for that wonderful little boy.

It was cool on this Sunday morning – 45 degrees. We went to church, then mowed the lawn and went to the Dairy Queen for supper. It was a good day.

Week 3

It's another beautiful morning, but the birds aren't singing. Why is that, I wonder. It was an odd day weather-wise….. vacillated between the sun shining, then cloudy, then raining – couldn't make up its mind, I guess. I started on Judy's quilt.

Temperatures in the 50s and foggy, but the sun promised to shine through all day. Shawn, Kevin, Sharon, and Seth went to Minneapolis this morning for a weekend with Rod's family. Gayle drove Roy and me to Hoyt Lakes to visit Don and Gerry who leave for Alaska on Tuesday. We had a wonderful visit and got home at 10:30.

We went to church and that's all. It's a very nice day (40 degrees with a high of 75 and no humidity) but there are so many mosquitos one can hardly be outside.

Week 4

Life goes on as usual. I thank and praise God for every day. Roy went to Thief River and then we went to Baudette for Bible study at Irene's…..it was a full and lovely day. Sharon got an A in her Criminal Justice course.

We picked plums at Marjorie Tveit's – huge, delicious plums. Joyce was out for a while and we had a good visit. The mornings are cool but the days are hot. I get up early to work on quilt blocks and then quit when it becomes hot and humid. I guess this is a sign of fall approaching.

Wayne and Pam worked on their yard while Joyce and Rod mowed ours. We were all together for Hannah's birthday party. How can I be lonely with such a great family and with knowing that God is always with me. I thank Him daily and ask Him to bless each and every one of my family, including those who live far away from here.

We went to church. Rozie's "end of summer" bonfire was a great success. It makes me feel good to see young people having fun!

Week 5

Fall is definitely around the corner…..gorgeous fall temperatures with cool evenings and warm days. We could use some rain. Zach went back to school at The University of Virginia and Willie moved to a new apartment in San Francisco, I think. Tony is in Bemidji this week. We don't see much of Gayle and Bill; they seem to be so busy travelling, golfing, etc.

I'm going to Inez's to start a new quilt, and then I'll can tomatoes. The temperatures dipped to 32 degrees but no frost yet. Hannah had her orientation for 7th grade….she's very excited. Where have all my children gone?!

Linsay and Matt came home; they had Lady with them. They all went camping at Hayes Lake. After church on Sunday, Joyce and Rod came out and we all visited with the campers at Hayes. I liked the Sunday message very much; it was on how God is our solid rock.

September – Week 1

Labor Day – a lovely day all around! Linsay and Matt went back to Duluth. Before he left, Matt helped Wayne and Pam rock my new flower bed; it looks so pretty. Gayle got as far as Watertown, South Dakota.

It's the first day of school for many of the grandchildren. How I pray that they will have a good year! Jon and Zach already have a week in; they both are taking heavy loads. I had my eyes checked in town......not much sight left in the left eye but the right one is very good. We also went to Warroad and had coffee with Joyce.

Another summer day of thunder and rain. I'm going to can tomatoes and, if it stops raining, I'll transplant some lilies. Gayle called from Fargo. She got home at 11:30. Praise God for His care! It's Wayne's birthday tomorrow. We're going to have a picnic at Penturen Church.

Week 2

Hannah had a home swim meet; Roseau lost to Warroad. It was fun to watch Hannah swim.....such a little fish. But then, we heard the horrible news of the attacks in New York and Washington, D.C. Oh, Lord, that people would forsake their terrible ways and seek Thee!

It's a beautiful day. I picked in some garden stuff and Roy is working to take down fencing up north. I talked to Jenny; she's all right, physically, but she sounded terribly sad. I keep paying that God will show His mercy to the poor people who are victims of the tragedy. Wayne painted the Quonset ends and his garage.

We went to church at 11:00 and then to Jena's birthday party at the park. It looks like rain.

Week 3

The terrorist attacks are still fresh in our minds and hearts. Oh, Lord, we need You – we cannot handle this terrible ordeal alone. I helped Roy take up fences up north; I drove the tractor and he worked hard to pull up the posts. I also washed four loads of clothes in between; they dried nicely. Inez and Bill brought out potatoes which we can use. Tony is home.

Helen needs prayer to get her through her latest ordeal. I pray for God's mercy to be given to Helen, and I pray that Louie and Dana will repent and come to you, oh, Lord. Amen.

We went to Thief River one day, and the next day we left for Duluth at 6:30 in the morning....Rozie drove. We went to Baby Jack's shower and had a good time with so many of my family. God, in His mercy, gave us a safe trip home. Praise Him, everyone!

Week 4

Oh, what another glorious morning! It froze hard last night but everything is so bright this morning. I must take up my geraniums and pot them for the winter. Fall is such a beautiful season…..beauty all around and no bugs or mosquitos. Wayne and Roy are working hard to get the new pasture ready. The cows are in the alfalfa….they must be watched closely or they'll eat until they bloat. God gives us the wisdom that we need. I ask Him daily to help me to keep my eyes on Him and then I thank Him for doing that. I'm working fiercely on Judy's quilt because I want to take it with me when we go.

I went with the ladies from the church to Thief River where we had lunch at the Scandia House….had a great time. Later in the day, Roy and I went with Gayle and Bill to the Fall Fest at Baudette and ate way too many potato pancakes. Dad, Mom, and Aunt Ruth used to make them for a treat and I hadn't had any for a long time. Joyce, Rod and family went with us, and we had a good time together.

We went to church and then attended David Slick's open house.

October – Week 1

The weather is still unbelievably nice! Roy is hauling hay. Tony came home for a couple of days. Inez and Millie came out so that we could work on Mama's things….a lot of reminiscing. Gayle, Bill and Pam had bean soup with us.

Roy went to Thief River on a very cold day. I dug up and carried everything from the garden to the deck that I wanted to save. Pastor Bill came over for coffee…..had a good time of conversation and prayer with him. I pray that God will bless all his efforts in our community.

It was very cold last night (19 degrees). Today is a clear and lovely fall day. I'm going to Sheltering Oaks to volunteer for a couple of hours. Wayne, Bill, Chris, Kevin, Rod and Joyce helped the vet test cows for pregnancy…..all but one are pregnant.

Such a wonderful day! We went to church and then Pam served a delicious chicken dinner and Hannah baked a cake for dessert……tasted so good. We had Bible study at Millie's afterward. Helen called me and I could tell that she was feeling a little better about the ordeal she's had to endure. Oh, Lord, help her and her family. Amen.

Week 2

Another beautiful day……Are we enjoying an Indian

Summer? I spent the time outside doing this and that. Wayne made a ditch and is now building a woodshed which is, of course, better than an ordinary shed (that's the way Wayne operates). He took in both cars to have them serviced for the winter; the Celebrity got two new tires.

I went to Bible study at Yvonne's this morning.....as always, it was so very good. Tony's friend, Jason, got a deer yesterday, the first one with a bow. The girls went to Grand Forks but I didn't go....it's just too much and I get tired easily. The old chickens went to a new home today....not Biddy though; Hannah would be despondent.

Last night we had our Harvest Festival at the church. It was a wonderful spiritual time. I look forward to that every year. That too has changed over the years. We used to bring bountiful gifts of our harvest to the minister and place them on the stage in front of the church. The free-will offering would be large, especially if the harvest had been good.

Joyce came out to wash the windows because it was such a nice day. Helen is doing so much better. God is answering my prayer for her.

Week 3

We left for Toledo early this morning. God was with

us all the way and the trip was uneventful. We had a great time being there with Judy and her family. She is such a lovely daughter and hostess – our wish was her command. Bill, too, is a dear and Jon included us in his daily life. His studies this semester are hard but he seems to have them under control most of the time. His social life is full, and he's using his violin to glorify God…….he makes such beautiful music! One of his friends was killed on Saturday, and he is so sad. She was talking on her cell phone and plowed into an oncoming car. So young, and her death seems so useless….. but who knows what good will come from the sadness. I pray that God will be involved in the healing process. We visited Salem Church where Judy is active in helping in any way she can. How wonderful that the love of Christ is shown to many in this way! We saw Clyde and Elaine, Mary Ann and Tom, and Loni and Mieko. We went to church with Judy, Bill and Jon. Jon played the violin so well – such a marvelous way to praise the Lord! It will be hard to leave this wonderful family in the morning.

Week 4

We stopped at Thief River on our way home and did some shopping. We got home at about 4:30 to a very cold and damp house – took all evening to warm up. Gayle and Bill brought supper over and Joyce had taken loads of laundry and rugs and washed them all. Oh, God, how blessed I am....so thankful! Wayne stopped over and Buford welcomed us exuberantly. I do appreciate the love and concern of my family.

Guess what – Christmas is here! We have four inches of wet snow and a beastly north wind......has winter started already?

The weather seems to be back to normal. I fried seven partridges today, went to Bible study at Inez's, and set up for the tea party at church on Sunday. The tea party turned out to be fun. I pray that the little cards with verses we made will bless each heart.

Week 5

Words that describe the weather this week: gorgeous, cold and raw, dreary, and glorious – all in one week. God knows we aren't ready for winter yet. I worked outside quite a lot during the nice days. Roy and I bought a car with the money I got from Mom and Dad. Rod says it's a good car, and it has everything. Phyllis and Mark are staying at Inez's, and Phyllis spent the day with me. Judy called; she is in Washington, D.C.

November 4th – hunting weekend: beautiful fall weather. Bill and the three boys arrived late. On the first day, Willie got two deer and Chris one with the bow and arrow. The second day Wayne and Hannah got one deer; Ryan one; Zach one; and Roz and Jon one. I baked pies for the hunters and we celebrated Kevin's birthday with cake and coffee at the shack. The women baked cookies for a cookie exchange, mostly at Gayle's. I enjoy spending time at the shack….such good company. I love my family so much, and God loves them even more.

November – Week 1

More beautiful Indian Summer weather……..I washed clothes and dried them outside; they smell so good! We made a quick trip to Warroad and then spent time with Inez and Phyllis. Wayne went to Minneapolis. I went to bed early and slept all night!

Esther's funeral was held on a wet, drizzly, chilly day. Evie, Irene and I spent the afternoon at Inez's. We had supper at the Pizza Place……..great companionship but not very good food. Phyllis and Mark left for home.

A gorgeous day again, a perfect day for waiting for a baby to arrive. Baby Jack will be here very soon, I hope. Roy and I had supper at the shack with the hunters. Why does food taste so delicious when it's cooked outdoors? Tony finally got his buck…..not the 30-pointer he was waiting for, but nice.

We went to church on a gorgeous day. Wayne, Pam, Roz and Hannah left early for Duluth. Chris got a nice buck. Hunting is officially over.

Week 2

It's a new week with a new baby! Jack was born at 2:30 a.m. – nine pounds plus. God bless him abundantly. The lovely weather continues. Roy and I had lunch with Joyce and Sharon, followed by Bible study in Roseau where I had a message from my Secret Pal…..it felt very good; I didn't know I had so many sore spots. I fixed venison for supper……it tasted very good.

I had my first asthma attack since last spring, so I didn't feel very well for a day. Wayne and Pam are having brick put on their house…….it looks very nice. Bill and Rod installed an early Christmas present – a new fridge. It's a beauty, but I hope that someone is enjoying my faithful old green one.

I slept around the clock and feel so much better. Willie called to thank us for his CARE package, and Jon called just to find out how we were. Shawn, Sharon, Jena and Seth came to see us; Seth has a very bad cough. Grandchildren are wonderful…..truly each one is a gift from God.

This morning, Yvonne and Bill thanked God for Jack's arrival and for Wayne and Pam's safe trip home.

Week 3

The gorgeous weather continues but it feels like November. Roy and I took a quick trip to Warroad for our flu shots. Hannah stayed home from school with strep throat; she's a pretty sick girl. Tony, Seth and Sharon are also not feeling well. Joyce came home from Minneapolis on the Marvin plane. We're having no Bible study this week. Arnie finished Wayne and Pam's house.

Thanksgiving – a wonderful holiday! Linsay, Matt, Josh and Katie are home. Thank you, God, for our darling little baby. Judy called (daily) to say that Clyde is preparing their turkey. Zach won't be home; he's in Charlottesville and will feast on spaghetti with Sweaty, his cat, as his guest.

After such beautiful sunny weather, today seems so gloomy……maybe we'll get some snow. The sermon was on forgiveness, something that everyone finds hard to do, I guess. Hannah and everyone else is feeling better. The Duluth people went home. Everyone does so much moving around these days and I'm forever grateful for safe travels.

Week 4

A cold, windy, dreary day with a promise of snow. I went with Roy to Thief River but felt so uncomfortable. As it turned out, it did snow – four inches. Wayne left for Minneapolis and I washed clothes and fried venison for Judy's family which I will take to Minneapolis this weekend. I also made her divinity and gingerbread......feeling a little bushed!

I had my hair done after Bible study on this gray day. I'm so looking forward to my Minneapolis weekend with the girls. Judy had foot surgery, so it will be interesting to see how she manages the weekend. Wayne came home from Minneapolis and Tony went there.

Annual Minneapolis weekend: Left the farm for Minneapolis at 6:30 this morning and met Joyce in Warroad – Pam couldn't go this year. Judy met us at the Hyatt – her foot is swollen but she handles it well. Oh, what a lovely time we had! Delicious meal while we watched an excellent production called "Simply Christmas." Went to a nearby casino afterward but that held no appeal for me. Saturday forenoon was leisurely and then Linsay, Matt, and little Jack spent the afternoon with us. Judy was thrilled to see them – we all were. Parade in the evening but I was so tired. We left at 10:00 on Sunday morning. Judy left at 2:00. Such a wonderful weekend, thanks to Judy and the girls. I am so blessed! We really missed Pam though.

December – Week 1

Days are short and nights are long now…..good time for hibernation. Roy seemed glad to have me home! We went to Warroad to deposit our checks…..saw Joyce, Sharon and Shawn who had a bad toothache. The weather is mild. Gayle went to Mahnomen but came home the same day. Wayne made delicious jerky. Bill is in Texas – Lord, give him a safe trip home. Pam delivered poinsettias from Judy.

The roads are very icy, due to the freezing rain, so I cancelled my appointments until next week. I can admit to my diary that I am not feeling well. I had my blood pressure checked two times and it is down….using asthma medication and it seems to help. The best I can do is give it to God, and He'll take care of it one way or another.

Praise God, Jon accepted Jesus as his Lord and Savior – officially. I've always sensed that he believed…..he's so kind and gentle. Lord, use him to further your kingdom and influence others. Thank you, Jesus – lead him, guide him and mold him. This is a day that the Lord hath made; we will lift Him up and rejoice in what He has done.

I'm better but still don't feel well. We went to the Christmas program at church......probably the last, or one of the last, for Hannah to participate in. It was very mild this morning – 20 degrees and a south wind. I pray that there will be no more rain to make ice.

Week 2

It's a little colder but certainly not a cold December for Minnesota. The days are long though, and I pray that God will lead me and show me how to use my time wisely. The doctors are keeping a close watch on my blood pressure. Wayne got a hefty check for the sale of his cattle, and Gayle came home from Minneapolis; Roy, Tony and I met her for lunch in Warroad. Tony did some Christmas shopping and then headed out to Ulvin's cabin to do some bow hunting.

The weather has warmed up again. It rained last night, and the snow is melting. I made divinity with Gayle; it didn't turn out to be very good, so I made another batch later on, and that was good. Dr. B. Anderson spoke at church...... his sermon turned out to be a nice fireside chat. Roy and I finished a pretty Thomas Kincaid puzzle. Willie called.

Week 3

The week began on a very mild and sunshiny note.......

thinking that spring had sprung early! Then it turned cold and dreary (five, then zero degrees). It's time to dress for winter; the long johns and extra sweaters feel good. I think I'm feeling some psychological effects from the weather vacillation......so disoriented, irritable and crabby. Help me, dear God, with my attitude.

So much traveling: Zach is going home from Virginia; Jenny and Jesse are traveling from New York; Katie, Matt, Linsay and Jack are driving from Duluth......God, drive for each one. And I pray for Willie whose world is fraught with uncertainty right now. Let him feel Your hand in leading him, Lord.

We are having a "picnic" at Joyce and Rod's tonight. One of the things we'll do is pack a Christmas box consisting of a meal to give away. Still no snow, but God still has three days to deliver.

We got a skiff of snow......about one half of an inch, just enough to whiten the landscape and fill my heart with joy. A white Christmas is something that everyone in Minnesota hopes for each year. Everyone got home safely.

Week 4

Christmas Eve at Pam and Wayne's....everyone helped and it was so good to be together. I kept thinking about Mama and how she would have loved the lutefisk because it was so firm and good. Wayne's and Gayle's families went to church at 11:00 – the midnight Christmas Eve service is special.

On Christmas Day, it was eight degrees below zero. We had a delicious brunch at Gayle and Bill's. Pam and Wayne and family went to Grand Forks; Lins, Matt and Jack returned to Duluth. Tony, Chris, Roy and Jesse went ice fishing – they caught 11 keepers, and we had a delicious supper of fresh walleye. I really like Jesse…..how I pray that he's the one for our Jenny.

Jenny and Jesse left on a morning when it was eight degrees but sunny and still. The roads here aren't bad, but I know that New York has an enormous amount of snow. I pray that they will have a safe trip.

We had our Clasen family Christmas this afternoon. I was a little disappointed that more young people weren't there, but we enjoyed everyone who did come. Cy, Irene, and Evie didn't come. Tracey and his family, Todd and his family, and Annette, Charles, Lynn and Brad and their two kids represented the young crowd.

2002 Journal Entries

January – Week 1

This is the last day of 2001….it's been quite a year! Nine eleven made a huge impact on our lives, and it's hard to forget that. Judy and her family had a great weekend at Boyne.....lots of snow and mild temperatures made for great skiing.

New Year's Day......certainly not January weather. The weather is unseasonal – makes me a little uneasy, but we enjoy the days filled with sunshine. Roy took all the men with him to clear the trail to Bemis Hill while the women stayed where it was warm and had good fellowship. The hot coffee warmed the men up when they had to leave. We had chili for supper at Pam and Wayne's.

Roy went to Thief River. Clayton Brandt was killed at the beginning of this week. How I grieve for Mavis – God help her in every way. The Warroad people started school today. We saw them briefly when we took our checks to the bank. I went to see Randa but she had broken her hip and wasn't home. I took down the Christmas tree because I didn't want Joyce to have to do it when she comes out tomorrow. I just hate to destroy Christmas trees. Rozie started school today.

I made a pot of bean soup and everyone who was here had a bowl. Gayle brought a cheesecake over so we had a feast and a good time together. I called Judy and her family. It's getting to be a habit being able to talk to her so often, but it's such a nice habit.

Week 2

It's a spring day in January – 40 degrees! We went with Gayle to Thief River for an appointment with the gynecologist who conducted some tests. She goes back next Thursday for the results.

High 28 degrees – lovely blue skies and sunshine. I washed clothes, sewed, and tussled. We had Bible study at Yvonne's......I'm so glad that it's started again after the December break. Rhonda's hip is healing and she was glad to see me. It's Jon's birthday.....he's 17 years old.

Wayne, Pam and Hannah went to Duluth. The girls are going shopping for Linsay's wedding dress, and the guys are going shopping at Menards (if Jack lets them). We had lunch with Joyce and family. Tony, friends, and Bill went fishing. Besides a nice catch of eating-size walleye, Tony caught his prize: a seven-to-eight-pound fish. I think he'll have it mounted.

Roy went fishing with the guys this morning – they had a nice catch. I went with Inez, Bill, Millie and Annette to Evie's for Bible study.....it was a very good afternoon. Wayne, Pam and the girls came home from Duluth about 8:00.

Week 3

It was 20 degrees above zero this morning.....Irene's

birthday. We had an uplifting time at Bible study yesterday. Zach flew to Spain to spend a semester of college there. I pray for him and for all my young people. I heard from Judy that his flight went well.

Our Grand Forks trip with the Bible study ladies was cancelled because of Evelyn Fausher's illness. A couple of days later we all got together – Gertie, Evelyn, Jodi, Yvonne and Pearl - and had a good time. Two days later, we managed our trip to Grand Forks to see Rose who is not good......has gone downhill a lot.

It's a nice, sunshiny day – not too cold. I went to Thief River with Gayle. Thanks be to God – she's okay! The doctor will decide this week what to do to help her with her problem. Jon aced his exams; God has something special in mind for Jonnie.

The Warroad people came out. We finished the lutefisk and had coffee and fresh rolls at Pam's – lots of talk about the upcoming wedding.

Week 4

This is an ordinary day, but it's beautiful – not cold, no wind, and snow falling so softly. It's a day that God has made and we rejoice and praise His holy name. I am so grateful for all my gifts from God, the most important being the love of my family, far and near. Zach called home and he's doing fine. Lord, be with him spiritually as well as physically. Oh, that people everywhere would open their eyes and see His goodness and His love for all mankind. I started a new puzzle.

It's colder today – 12 degrees this morning. After Bible study, I visited with Margaret Lindholm and Berta Kronberg – both are very dear to me. They will both be 90 sometime this year. I had to promise them that I would bring Judy to visit the next time she was home. I also saw Randa yesterday. She was very distraught and on a real roll. How can I help her? God will have to touch her somehow and I pray that He will. I haven't heard from "the girls" for some time.

The men went fishing today…..they caught some real nice ones. Hannah spent the afternoon with me. I enjoyed having her so much. We baked, played games and served Gayle coffee. We closed out the day with a fish fry…..there's almost nothing better than walleye from the frozen water. I didn't feel well last night and it's catching up with me so I'll probably go to bed early.

And I end this year as it began: praising God for His mercy, love and faithfulness to all of us. If we ask Him to come to us, He will……..maybe not the way we want Him to, but His will is better anyway!

Chapter 9
2003, 2004

(2003 and 2004 calendar summaries)

"I know the plans I have for you," declares the Lord, "plans to prosper and not to harm you, plans to give you hope and a future. Then, you will call on me and come and pray to me, and I will listen to you. You will seek me and find me, when you seek me with all your heart."
Jeremiah 29: 11-13

2003 Calendar Summary

The first entry for January: "Roy predicts that in two years no snocats will be built." I think he made that prediction based on the warm weather they were experiencing at the beginning of the month. Jenny and Jesse's wedding was beautiful and a good time was had with everyone being there on the farm. The Patbergs returned to Toledo on January 3rd, and the Clasens gathered for their Christmas at Inez's

The Years Come and Go

church that weekend. It was 40 degrees with melting snow on January 7th, and that spring-like weather continued for a few days, until the temperatures dropped to 20 below, then 30 below on Super Bowl Sunday (the 26th), but ended the month above zero again (20 degrees). For some reason, Mom kept track of when the heat was off.......recording the hours for each day during the cold weeks. The heater in the dog house went out on the 20th, and the water froze on the 22nd. Mom had a mammogram on January 30th. The cows began a new sack of oats on January 1st.

February's weather appeared to be fairly typical: temperatures ranging from 15 above to 35 below, with beautiful sunny days and a few snowy, windy days. Mom continued to track off peak which was, at one point, off almost all day and part of the night. Phyllis and Robert visited for a few days, and the annual Boyne ski trip on Presidents' Day had everyone leaving for a long weekend. Dad went to Thief River on the 25th.......a very cold day.

Ten little calves were born and one cow died in March, a month which began on a cold note with temperatures in the ten to 25 below zero range and then warmed up to 55 degrees above zero one day. It snowed throughout the month with Warroad receiving 12 inches on the 27th. Fifty pounds of corn lasted four months, and a new bag was started on the 7th.

Judy spent a week on the farm at the beginning of the month; Katie, Linsay and Jack came later; and Mary and Cy's visit closed out the month. Off peak was off most of the month. Mom got her hair done on March 26th.

Mom noted that Judy was home from a conference in Dallas on April 1st. Seth's birthday was celebrated on the 6th, which was a beautiful day with 20 degrees of sunshine. Katie came home for Easter, followed by Matt, Linsay and Jack the next weekend. The weather for both visits – and for the entire month – was gorgeous with temperatures ranging from 20 to 60 degrees, reaching 80 degrees on Palm Sunday. Five inches of snow fell on April 3rd and then three inches on the 17th. Mom washed clothes and hung them outside on the 7th; planted 25 onions on the 21st; and had to deal with a painful bout of arthritis during the last week. A little calf was born during Easter week.

The merry month of May brought temperatures in the 40s and 50s with a couple of days in the 20s (froze a little) and 70s. The weather alternated between sun and rain with some wind mixing things up. Dad painted the house; the kids cleaned the house; and Tony began a "very good job." Jon began his summer job as a dishwasher and busboy at a country club. The cows resided in the south pasture with the bull. June brought warmer weather with temperatures in the

70s and 80s, except for the fourth week when they dropped into the 60s. Strong hot winds competed with a strong north wind and it rained several days. Mom noted that Judy and Jon were back home (no information as to where they had been). Mom and Dad spent a week in Toledo at the beginning of the month. The cows had been moved to the southwest pasture.

Wayne, Pam and Hannah went to Duluth the first week in July while the rest of the family celebrated the Fourth in Warroad.......not surprisingly, Mom enjoyed the parade the most. It was a hot week – 85 degrees – but the wind switched to the north and cooled things off so that by the 8th, it was 40 degrees in the morning. Fair week was beautiful.....very dry with warm days and cool nights. The cows didn't move from the southeast pasture. Little Morgan visited Mom and Dad on July 30th, and Mom decided to accompany Gayle on her census duties. The month ended with unsettling weather: lots of rain and strong winds.

Extreme heat (90s) characterized most of August.....part of which was hot and humid and the other part hot and dry. A little calf was born on one of those hot days. Temperatures moderated the last week so that it was 40 degrees in the morning and 60 degrees during the days.

Note: Mom included a note that she had clipped to the August calendar: 2003 has been the very best summer I can remember. Spring was early and the weather all summer long was ideal. NO MOSQUITOS…….not any, and very few flies! The farmers had a bumper crop.

The lovely weather continued in September with 65 degrees and a healthy amount of rain. Then it became hot and rainy (90 degrees) followed by cool and rainy……. "unsettled," Mom called it. On the first day of autumn, temperatures fell to the 40s and lower 50s, accompanied by rain and frost at night. The Penturen Church hosted the Sunday service on the 21st. The cows traveled from the southwest to the southeast pastures and settled down in the east pasture. A note on the calendar at the beginning of the month is ambiguous: "Building on Stuga; Fred worked Raymond's house and Alfred's."

Gorgeous! It's an adjective that Mom used to describe the weather for the first two weeks of October. Then it turned chilly….. "typical fall weather," Mom called it. She had her hair done on the 14th. Mom and Dad left for Toledo on the 21st and they, along with Judy and Jon, took a side trip to San Francisco to see Willie who "took us to see so many wonderful things such as the amazing Sequoias." They returned to Toledo and then went home on the 29th. During their time away, Wayne shipped 15 calves, and three to four inches of snow fell on the farm, while eight inches fell in other places.

Bill, Jon and Zach joined the group on November 7th for opening deer hunting this year. It was a cold weekend (ten below to 20 above) with about five inches of snow and at least one day of sun. The group shot three deer, and Chris got another one the next weekend. November 11th was an "absolutely gorgeous day" with temperatures in the 20s. The snow was gone by the 17th when the thermometer registered 35 degrees. Thanksgiving was held at Sharon's and Joyce's......it was 12 degrees in the morning. The toilet flushed on November 29th, a day before the "kids" (Jenny, Katie and Roz) returned home.

The annual Minneapolis weekend was mild, but the temperatures dropped the following week (28 below) with six inches of snow on the ground. Christmas week was very mild with temperatures in the high 30s and 20s. Hannah had appendicitis surgery on December 23rd, and Katie left for Colorado on New Year's Eve.

2004 calendar summary

It was a consistently cold January. Temperatures ranged from 20 above to 20 below until the last week when the thermometer was stuck at 30 to 40 below zero. On January 30th, it was 45 degrees below zero, and the car wouldn't start. Snow accumulation recorded for the month was 13 and a half inches. On January 20th, a winter storm closed all the schools and most of the businesses. Joyce had Bible study on January

11th. Mom's charitable donations for the month were sent to Samaritan's Purse, Teen Challenge, St. Jude's, Boys of Omaha, Campus Crusade for Christ, and one other called "Union."

February temperatures were mostly above zero…..in the 20s. Brandon's funeral was held on the coldest day of the month when it was 30 below. Beautiful weather (20 above) in the middle of the month brought out the snocats, and there were several trips to Bemis Hill and surrounding areas. Irene had Bible study on the 8th; Judy came home on the 16th; and the family enjoyed a fish fry on the 29th. Two little calves were born during the end of the month. Mom had several doctor appointments: February 4th (mammogram), the 16th (biopsy in Grand Forks), and two in Fargo on the 13th and the 17th (angiogram). She donated to the same charities she had donated to in January.

Mom recorded the births of ten little calves in March, one of which died on the 16th. Inez broke her ankle on March 1st when it was very slippery due to snow and rain. For most of the month the temperatures were in the high teens, 20s, and low 30s; the exceptions were March 10th when it was 35 degrees and the 24th when it was 48 degrees, followed by 55 degrees the next day. Mom and Dad planted seeds on that day. There fell a considerable amount of snow in the middle of the month. Mom had a doctor's appointment in Fargo

The Years Come and Go

on March 9th and saw Dr. Herseth the next day. She had an overnight hospital stay on the 19th and a stress test on the 29th, a cold and windy birthday for Dad.

The tulips raised their little heads on April 6th, a beautiful 65-degree day. Wayne went to Minneapolis on the 5th; Seth's birthday was celebrated on the 18th; and Annette had Bible study on the 24th. The Duluth group, as well as Judy and family, arrived at the farm in time for Easter, which was a chilly day for hiding and hunting eggs (15-20 degrees). Temperatures for the month ranged from 30 degrees to 60 degrees, with a normal amount of rainfall. Mom wrote "Is everything frozen?" on the 22nd.

Mom must have been especially conscientious about the weather in May because she recorded the details of every day. On May 1st, it was 20 degrees in the morning with a north wind and a high of 45. Two days later, the south wind turned east and it rained. The sun shone brightly on the 4th and continued to do so for a few days. May 8th was clean-up day on the farm, and it was a beautiful 72 degrees. The balmy weather turned cold on the 11th when it rained and snowed all day. The rest of the month turned out temperatures mostly in the 30s and 40s and rain mixed with sun. On May 17th, Mom recorded: "It's a beautiful day. The goldfinches are here......so is a red breasted gross beak and a Baltimore

Oriole!" Hannah was confirmed on the 16th. Mom and Dad planted corn on the 22nd when it was 65 degrees. A little calf was born on the 20th when a light frost covered the pasture. The cows munched in the southwest, west, east and south pastures. The bull broke out on the 19th. Mom made her monthly charitable donations.

June produced cool, wet weather in the middle of the month, along with 38 degrees and a touch of frost the fourth week. Other than that, the temperatures settled in the 50s and 60s with some 70-degree days, culminating in a high of 85 on June 29th. Mom went to Fargo on June 8th and had a mastectomy the next day. The cows traveled from the east pasture to the south and on to the barn-corral pastures and ended the month in the southeast pasture. Mom had a perm on the 4th, and Dad planted tomatoes for himself and Wayne on the 30th.

July temperatures ranged from 50 to 85 degrees with frequent, but not huge amounts, of rain. "Lovely weather!" Mom wrote. Pam and Wayne went to Duluth, and the "kids" camped one night at Tony's. Wayne cut hay on the 9th, the day before a bad storm hit Williams and Sprague. Mulehead's calf was born on July 21st when the thermometer recorded 84 degrees. Mom added "Feed the Children" to her list of charitable donations, and she ordered "Country" for Judy,

"Guideposts" for Margaret, and "Reader's Digest" for Roy. The bull flies arrived on July 19th......but not in large numbers. She had an oncologist appointment on the 30th, which she labeled a "total waste."

"The gang's all here!".......Mom's first comment on the August calendar. Everyone, including the Patbergs, apparently stayed for a week at the beginning of the month. Morgan celebrated her birthday with a party on the 8th. The weather was beautiful for the last two weeks of the month with temperatures in the 70s.......frost on the 19th. The cows resided in the south pasture, then the west pasture, then back to the south where a little calf was born on the 31st. The beautiful summer weather continued into September when the tomatoes started ripening on the 12th, the same day that Pam and Wayne, Joyce and Rod, and Katie left to join Judy in Norway. It was 90 degrees on September 19th, and then frost killed the cucumbers on the 27th. The cattle were in the west and east pastures. Gerry's name was on the calendar for the 14th, and Phyllis's name appeared on the 23rd with a question mark.

Mom's October calendar was barebones with a few vague comments about the weather (nice day, cloudy and rainy, 57 degrees) and a note about the trip she and Dad took to Toledo and Oklahoma on the 5th, returning on the 19th. The

November calendar, on the other hand, was filled with news of events and the weather, which was generally lovely...... "summer weather," Mom called it. It was a beautiful 50 degrees when Bill arrived for the opening deer weekend. Jack celebrated his birthday at the shack when it was sunny and 20 degrees in the morning. Alfred's funeral was held on the 12th. Phyllis and Trish arrived on the 19th and stayed at Mom and Dad's. Katie and Linsay came home for Thanksgiving. Gayle and Bill must have gone somewhere because Mack was with Mom and Dad.

December arrived on a very raw and windy note but then turned sunny and still (12 degrees) for the Minneapolis weekend. Rain and ice cancelled church on the 12th, and it was ten degrees below zero on the 13th with lots of sunshine. For the rest of the month, temperatures ranged from 15 above to one day when it was 30 below. Christmas week was very cold and sunny. Rozie, Katie, Lins and Jack came home for Christmas. On New Year's Eve it was 18 degrees and four to five inches of snow fell.

Note: Mom kept two calendars for 2004, one that carried most of the news and another that recorded her charitable contributions and a few medical appointments. What is odd about the second calendar is her handwriting: in some instances, it is hard to read.......one possibility is that her left hand wasn't working well, perhaps because of arthritis, so she wrote the entries using her right hand.

Chapter 10
2005, 2006

(2005 journal entries and calendar summary and 2006 journal entries and calendar summary)

Pray always. Pray in the Spirit. Pray about everything in every way you know how! And keeping all this in mind, pray on behalf of God's people. Keep on praying fervently, and be on the lookout until evil has been stayed.
Ephesians 6:18

Whatever you ask in prayer, you will
receive, if you have faith.
Matthew 21:22

2005 Journal Entries

October 29

My first entry is a sad one. My beloved sister Phyllis is dying.

November 7

Sometimes I feel so far away from God. I'm not one to commit murder or extortion or any of those acts of sin that reach headlines in the paper. But I realize that I'm a sinner because of the little daily things that keep me from Him – such as crabby words that I utter to those around me or failure to act when God speaks to me (because I am too proud?) or not carrying out my routine daily duties as I should. I know that these sins keep me from entering God's presence. Lord, forgive me, the chief among sinners. Amen.

November 29

My beloved sister Phyllis, has died – she who was always so full of life. I pray for Phyllis' family as they grieve for her. Praise God…..He saw fit for her to leave. Jesus said, "Come home, dear one," and He took her by the hand and away they went. "I'm ready to go home," she said, "Jesus paid it all for me." What a blessed comfort to my soul! Everyone, wherever you are, come to Jesus and He will not turn you away.

I am so happy for Katie and Bill. I firmly believe that God brought them together. I pray for Bill's safety in Iraq (others also). What a horrible war – so blood thirsty on both sides! I pray not only for his physical return but, Lord, mentally, psychologically, and spiritually as well.

Note: Mom is talking about Katie and Bill's official wedding. They had their lovely, traditional, family wedding over a year later after Bill returned from Iraq.

December 15

I feel so "undone" this morning. I am anxious! I read Psalm 91, written by David in times of trial. I have no trial and I surely am not facing tribulation. I am taking verses 14-16 as my own. I am going to trust him every hour of the day. Thank you, Lord, for your Word.

Note: "Because he hath set his love upon me, therefore will I deliver him; I will set him on high, because he hath known my name. He shall call upon me, and I will answer him; I will be with him in trouble; I will deliver him, and honor him. With long life will I satisfy him, and show him my salvation." Psalm 91: 14 - 16

2005 Calendar Summary

On January 1st, there were five to six inches of snow on the ground, and it was zero degrees. The temperature dropped over the next few days......minus 12, minus 24, minus 27, and minus 38. Another five to six inches of snow fell. Bible study was cancelled, but the funeral for R. Gust took place. For the rest of the month, temperatures ranged from 20 below to 25 above, with sunshine on many days and blowing snow from a strong wind on others. February began on a considerably warmer note with temperatures in the 20s and 30s...... several 35-degree days. "Some very cold weather took over here" while the gang was skiing at Boyne. All the plants that Mom kept upstairs froze. Temperatures moderated during the last few days of the month when the sun shone and it snowed lightly. Mom received a very good report on her eyes.

Eleven calves were born in March and one calf died. It appears that March came in like a lion and went out like a lamb. In between, the weather featured gorgeous warm, sunny days (23 to 39 degrees) and cold, blustery, overcast days (minus 15 degrees to zero degrees). On March 31st, the temperature was 50 degrees......... "Glorious!" Mom said. Linsay and Jack spent a weekend on the farm and Pam, Wayne, and Hannah went to Duluth for Easter.

Mom planted some flower seeds the first of April, a day that featured a morning temperature of 25 degrees and a high of 50 degrees. The first two weeks of the month appeared to be lovely with temperatures as high as 75 degrees and sunny. Then, it turned colder and the rain descended. The snow disappeared on April 10th when the water was drying up and the daffodils were sprouting. On April 18th, it was 85 degrees; on the 22nd it was 45; and it snowed on the 30th. A little calf was born on the 24th. Judy spent the very cold last week of the month on the farm.

Snowy, rainy and cold: These were the weather descriptors for the first days of May. What followed appeared to be a month that was indecisive as far as the weather was concerned. A day when it was 70 degrees and sunny made room for one where the high was 45 degrees with rain and wind (but no frost at night). This pattern continued until the last three days of the month that Mom labeled "Beautiful! Gorgeous! Sunny!" A little calf was born on the 15th and another on the 25th. The bull got out on the 28th. Gayle and Bill went to New York on the 18th, and Mom had her hair done. On May 30th, she wrote "Fred worked the field again."

It rained the first eight days of June. Then, June 9th produced a beautiful blue sky with white, puffy clouds and a temperature of 70 degrees, while June 14th turned out a wet, dark and drizzly day with two inches of rain. Most of the rest of the month was sunny and very warm, with the thermometer registering 95 degrees on the 23rd. The family enjoyed a fish fry on June 11th; and Wayne cut hay on the 25th. The cows were pasture-hopping: southeast, east, and west.

Kittson County endured a flash flood – ten to 15 inches – on July 3rd, when only three quarters of an inch fell on the farm. Wayne hayed during the July 4th week......bailed hay on the 10th and he and Dad cut some more on the 12th and 13th. The weather for most of the month was beautiful – hot with temperatures in the 80s and 90s and no rain. Six inches of rain fell in a thunderstorm on July 30th. Two calves were born in July, one of which was Mulehead's. Hot temperatures in the 90s began the month of August, but cooler temperatures prevailed for the rest of the month (70s). Mom labeled August a "month of lovely weather." Anthrax was discovered in Leroy's pasture at the beginning of the month. Five inches of rain fell in Warroad and Lake Bronson on the 17th. The weather was perfect for our family party on the 27th. Mom made note of Judy and Jon's arrival for the party, followed by Bill, Zach, and Willie. Everyone left on the 28th. Rozie left for somewhere on the 30th (probably for her nannying job in New Jersey). The cows enjoyed the east and southwest pastures during the month.

Note: Mom was referring to the surprise party at Bemis Hill that all of us organized for Mom and Dad's 80th birthdays. Their arrival at the party produced the quintessential Roy and Margaret photo that's featured in this book.

September was marked by more lovely weather (50s and 60s with sunshine for many of the days) but also by some bad news about the cows, including Mulehead. A camping trip had to be cancelled for the weekend of the 4th because

The Years Come and Go

of strong thunder. Jack spent a few days on the farm and went home on the 9th. Bible study was held at Irene's on the 18th, and church services took place at Penturen on the 25th. On the 30th of September, Mom recorded a morning temperature of 45 degrees and proclaimed that it was "going to be a lovely day."

Mom began the October calendar with one of her famous ambiguous notes: "Beautiful day at camp." There was a horrible blizzard in North Dakota and flooding in Minneapolis and St. Paul on the 5th and 6th of October. The farm had one and a half inches of rain and a hard frost. For the next three weeks – and the remainder of the month – the weather was lovely: sunny and very mild. Pam and Wayne left for Duluth on the 8th and Mom and Dad for Toledo on the 13th.

The calendar events of November included Travis's baptism, Gayle's Bible study, and Katie's wedding. Mom and Dad went to Duluth with Pam and Wayne for the wedding and endured a horrendous ride home because of an ice storm that made the roads almost undrivable. Mandy and Chris went in the ditch and had to stay overnight somewhere. November temperatures ranged from 55 degrees to 30 degrees and snow fell during the opening deer hunting weekend. There were about four inches of snow on the ground on the 18th. November appeared to be a quite cold month.

Except for a very mild stretch during Christmas week, December was an unpredictable weather month with temperatures ranging from highs of 30 degrees to minus ten degrees; a fair amount of snow fell quietly and steadily. Jenny and Andrew were on the farm for the second week of December. Christmas Day featured temperatures in the lower 30s for the high. Mom had her hair done on December 9th in preparation for the holidays.

2006 Journal Entries

January 1

I just read a wonderful piece of advice. "Trust Me, I have everything under control," said Jesus. If I can just remember this little line of encouragement today and throughout the new year – whatever it brings – I will be at peace. Lord, thank you for that promise. Amen.

Home is where the family gathers, where the family grows and where they give to each other. It need not be elegant or fancy if there is love. Someone said this and I think it's a wonderful thought.

Well, the new year came in with very mild weather. The temperature is 20 degrees and no moisture. After church today, the Clasen group is meeting for a little holiday party. I made some potatoes (but cooked them too long…..what else is new?) and rice (which should be good).

Wayne and Pam left yesterday for Duluth to spend the weekend with their own family and to see Roz off on the plane back to New Jersey. I wonder if they watched the new year come in. I talked to Judy……..she and Bill watched the ball drop in Times Square. They are spending the weekend with John and Dee. Today they are meeting Zach, Jenny, Jesse and Drew in New York.

I thank God for another year and for each day that He gives me. With His help, I'll try to live each new day pleasing Him.

January 9

Today is Jon's birthday. He's 21 years old. Now both he and Rozie are part of the "mature" group. I pray that he will have a good day.

The weather remains mild with a little snow now and then. A winter like this surely makes "living" easier although I do long for a cold day or a blizzard now and then.

We had Bible study at Evie's yesterday. I pray, Lord, that seeds were sown and that You watered them among us. Irene wasn't feeling well at all; I hope she's better this morning. Her wrist is feeling fine. God, be with her and hold her in Your arms.

Hannah is working quite a lot these days and I think she likes having her own money – the little Sweetie. Tony is gone a lot to see Jenny in the Fargo area. I pray that she appreciates him and loves him as he does her. We hear from Judy almost every day and keep in touch with those nearby. How lonely we would be without them! God bless each one.

January 14

My heart is crying out to Gerry, my sister who had to make the hard decision to leave her husband. Be with her, God, and give her the courage to do what's right. Isaiah 63:9 – "In His love, He lifted them up and carried them." Thank you, Jesus.

The warm, wet and rainy weather continues. One day January and winter will come. Tony has been in Fargo all week. I miss him stopping by.

January 19

Praise God for another day! Tony came home but he has a bad sore throat. He went to get medication yesterday…..I hope it isn't strep. (Turns out it wasn't.) It turned a little colder – seven degrees below zero. Now that still isn't January but it definitely feels like winter.

Joyce continues to enjoy her job. Last week they bonded her so that she can drive the school vehicle. Now she uses that to transport the students who live east of Salol and they can go right home – no need to use her own car. I pray that Shawn will find a good job also. Sharon continues to like hers and feels secure in it. I continue to pray for each of "my children" daily that God will bless each one spiritually as well as physically. And I know that He hears my cry for them all.

I haven't heard from many since Christmas so all must be well. Judy continues to call almost every day. She spent last weekend at Boyne getting ready for the big ski weekend. Wayne continues to stop by for coffee. How I will miss that when he no longer stops in.

January 29

January is almost over! Usually it is such a long, slow month, but it has been so mild and probably that's why it seems not to have dragged on – actually, it appears to have flown! It remains very mild (20 degrees) this morning. I learned the other day that this mild winter is caused by the jet stream that remains way up north and won't let the cold air south….usually it fluctuates but it's not ready to do so yet.

Linsay has been very sick but she seems to be rallying. I pray that she'll consult with the doctor tomorrow and maybe they'll be able to determine the cause. Our prayers are constant for her.

Katie called and gave us good news from her and Bill – a new little life is on the way. Bless this little soul, Lord, and bless Katie and Bill. Help them to be good parents to this little one that you have entrusted to them.

Tony and Roy have been cutting firewood for Wayne this week – a few hours every day. Tony drove to Fargo for the weekend to be with Jenny. I pray for both of them.

February 4

Today we got what we've been waiting for – winter! It's 20 degrees below zero – quite a shock! This is the day that the Lord has made and we will rejoice and be glad in it.

Yesterday Judy and I were talking about faith, and this morning my devotions were on faith! Faith does not mean that we should stop thinking. We need to trust in Him at all times, but that doesn't mean we can drive carelessly or spend money like it's going out of style or become slovenly or apathetic. We can't expect God to bail us out when we are being foolish. That's not faith. Hebrews 11:6 – "He who comes to God must believe that He is and that He is a rewarder of all who seek Him." Thank you, Lord.

February 20

It's a beautiful day (20 degrees) and it's snowing……..not hard but steadily. It makes for a good day. We've had such cold weather! Last week it was 35 degrees below zero. The cattle watering system froze up but with the help of Tony and Bill, it thawed out – lots and lots of boiling water was used.

Wayne and Pam, Katie, Linsay, Jack, Hannah, Jena, Joyce and Rod are skiing at Boyne. They are supposed to be home this evening. It will be good to have them all back again. They have had a very good time with Willie and Jenny, Jesse and Jenny and Andrew, Jonathan, Judy and Bill. Tomorrow it's back to work for everyone. Gayle, Bill and Tony didn't go to Boyne and we were very happy to have them here.

February 28

So let's live today to the fullest because it's such an important ordinary day. Most of my days are just ordinary ones, dull and uninteresting. But if I remember that "this is a day that the Lord has made" and trust Him in all things, then it becomes an important ordinary day.

The last day of February – tomorrow we look ahead for Spring to arrive…..it will be a while yet here in northern Minnesota, but it is coming. I wonder: What have I done to serve the Lord this past month? What have I done to serve Him today? He knows me inside and out. Is He pleased with me? I am so very thankful that Jesus is my Savior and Redeemer. I can give to Him all my sins and shortcomings, and His blood will wipe them all away. Thank you, God, for Jesus; I need Him every hour of every day.

March 1

Well, the skiers are all here and they had a wonderful time at Boyne. February is over, and I read that this February was colder than normal (compensating for January which was a warmer than normal month). Anyway, time marches on and we along with it.

Yesterday was such a gorgeous day. Roy and I went for a little ride to Bemis Hill and to see all the cutting on the Tofte Trail. The roads were good until the last part. We got stuck in nowhere land with no shovel, no cell phone – just us. Roy decided to walk back to where some cutting had been done. Sure enough, with God's leading, Roy found a camp that was active. A very nice young man pulled us out with his four-wheel drive pickup – no charge! Meanwhile, I was preparing myself for a long wait in the car until help would come. I did a lot of praying for patience and knew that God would provide all that we needed. So I thanked Him, praised Him and promised to worship Him with all my heart.

It's supposed to snow a lot today. Maybe March is coming in like a lion?

March 13

It has snowed a lot. Today it is cold, five degrees this morning. The sun is out though and it promises to be a very nice day. We have two baby calves – so cute! Wayne succeeded in getting the cows near the barn, and that gave him much peace of mind. Thank you, Lord, for helping us with our daily problems of living.

Freddy is not well – his lungs are giving him big problems. Robert Slick had a stroke that paralyzed his left side and affected his speech. Oh, Lord, be with these two men. Speak to their hearts for spiritual healing and touch their bodies with physical healing.

Your day, Lord! Help me, help us to listen to what You have to say. "Under His Wings" is my song today.......I will safely abide forever! My heart is so full this morning! First of all, it's so full of thanksgiving and praises for Your great mercy to us, your ever-present love for us. I pray that You will be ever - present with Freddy. Keep him under Your wings, Lord. And for Robert….that You will be with him, Holy Spirit; change his heart. For Shawnie, as she starts her new job…..oh, Lord, that she'll lean on You for without You, Lord Jesus, her efforts will be to no avail. For Judy, as she works with this organization for the lost, the "throw-aways" of society. Bless them, Lord, as they seek Your face in all that they do. For again, Lord, it is You that saves us – we can do nothing without You. Bless us all, old and young, as we give ourselves to You.

Judy is coming on Wednesday. Give her a good trip, Lord.

April 11

Easter week! Blessed be the name of the Lord…..He is so good! What more can one give than to give to us His son, Jesus, who gave His life for us, who shed His blood that has the power to cleanse us from all sin – Jesus, who is alive and provides a way for us to come to the Heavenly Father – for without Him we cannot enter Heaven. Thank you, God, for the wonderful gift of salvation. And so, I will praise Him and worship Him. Oh, that people everywhere will take that wonderful gift, unwrap it, and accept it for themselves.

Much has happened in the month since Judy was here. She had a little trouble getting here because of cancellations, etc.

But we had such a great week together, and Roy and I miss her so much when she isn't here.

Spring is truly here. All things are coming to life. Little buds of new life are poking up everywhere. The tulips, crocuses, daffodils, and much more are peeking through and, with the warm weather, are growing fast. The buds of trees are slower but they also will come. Little calves are being born. We have one little bottle calf to feed and he is growing. The other day, twins were born but only one lived. Truly, it is a wonderful time of the year! Winter, with its darkness and cold, is past and we are "coming alive" again in the warmth of the sun.

May 13

"Bless This House".......my song for this morning. Am I a follower of Jesus Christ or am I trying to be a leader and have Him follow me? Oh, Lord, help me to follow You each day. Lead me in Your path......Your will be done! You have told us to seek Your face and pray for those around us. But, Lord, help me to know, beyond a shadow of a doubt, that it is You who is in command. Amen.

The last few days have been unpleasant – cold and damp, and yet everything is growing and flourishing. But my spirit for gardening has sunk to a new low.

May 14

The calf situation is just about at a standstill. The little bottle calf is growing, but he has a malady of one of his front knees. We are treating it but it doesn't seem to become smaller – thus, he can't walk very well.

Linsay was home for a couple of days to fix Hannah's hair for the prom, but she was quite sick so she couldn't enjoy the festivities. Both Hannah and Jena looked beautiful.

Last week Katie and Jack came home for a few days. The baby is making itself evident and Katie is feeling well. Jack went home on Tuesday, but Katie stayed until yesterday. She and Sitka drove to Stillwater before she heads to Duluth.

Jenny and Andrew also arrived last weekend and are leaving this afternoon. They are riding to the Grand Forks airport with Tony's Jenny who is working in Austin, Minnesota this month. I get to feeling very low when everyone leaves. Coming and going – that's life and it's a real blessing!

There is a baby shower for little Natalie Eaton this afternoon…….should be fun.

May 22

And that cold weather continues. It froze hard the other

night, but today it looks as if a turning point has come. I think things won't be permanently damaged but it was cold. I'm going to set out the plants today…..they need to be outside.

What a glorious morning! The sun is shining; the birds are singing; and my spirits are soaring! It's funny how our spirits rise on a morning like this! Thank you, Lord, for this new day. I know that every day is a day that the Lord has made, and I do thank and praise Him for each one. This morning, though, seems special. I pray that the Lord will help me to remember that my strength and my help come from Him.

The bottle calf is doing well. His knee is deformed but he's frisking about. Joyce and Rod were out for a while and we saw the little fox who have their den just outside the pasture. They're very cute and growing. I wish they would leave the farmyard though and go into the wild where they belong.

Freddy and Leroy are getting the fields planted. I think that Leroy and Arlan are doing most of the work. Freddy is better but not doing well. Thank you, God, for being with him. Thank you also for healing Bill and for helping Robert to recover from the stroke that he suffered late this winter. The rest of the family is faring well, as far as I know.

Bill "took the bull by the horns" one day and started putting a roof on the deck. This is something I've wanted for a long time. On Saturday, Wayne helped him and now all that is left to do is shingle it. I know that Roy and I are going to enjoy it a lot.

Pam, Wayne, and Hannah are going to Duluth this next weekend for a work-related time. They are going to help Linsay set up her little garden and do other chores around her place. Katie and the baby are doing fine; Bill misses being with them.

Jena has golf play-offs this week. I know she is nervous about it, but she'll do well.

June 12

We've had a cold week but it's also been very pleasant….. the nights have been chilly but no frost.

Rozie was home this week – what a joy! She brought Mark out to meet us. He certainly wasn't what I expected…… seemed to be shy. He's expecting to be deployed to Iraq sometime this summer. I pray for him and for all the young men who have to go to Iraq. It's a very dangerous situation and it doesn't seem to be getting any better. We'll do what we can do, but what happens when we have no control over it. Thank God, He is sovereign!

The garden looks good. There's been no rain for many

days so it is very dry…..we have to water frequently to make sure it has enough moisture. The pastures are still producing good grass and feed for the cattle, but the hay isn't growing very fast. Maybe it will rain this week.

Hannah and Jena are spending this week with Judy, Bill and Jon. Jena had her golf tournament (did well) and left for Toledo from Minneapolis.

June 20

Everyone seems to have gotten home safely. Judy and Bill will be flying home from San Francisco either late tonight or early tomorrow. Judy says San Francisco is a nice place to be, and Willie and Jenny enjoy living there. Now this noon, Wayne is driving to the Cities and will be back tomorrow. The Lord has been caring for us each hour of every day. With all the traveling going on, He promises to be with each one. I'm so glad He's in control and I thank Him every day.

God sent us a much-needed rain over the weekend. How I pray that rain will fall on South Dakota where the drought is so prevalent. Many times I feel so frustrated with conditions around the world. What can I do to help? Then He reminds me that I can pray. I am me, the only me in all the world and God has a purpose for me. Lord, help me to keep my eyes fixed on you.

Linsay completed the half marathon in Duluth. About 16,000 people participated and she finished in the top half…..about 350th place, I think.

Wayne started haying last evening after work. He is cutting on Leonard Carlson's. Life goes on day by day and tomorrow will be the first day of summer…..we'll soon be on the down swing again.

August 1

Much has happened since I last wrote. Wayne has basically finished haying. Leonard Carlson asked him to bale up some green oats he planted…..Wayne can keep the bales. He has plenty of hay but, because of the extremely hot and dry season, he probably will start feeding the cattle early.

July was so beastly hot and dry…..records were set! Many days it was in the 90s or close to it. The gardens are not good, even with hand-watering. Even the beans didn't produce. The tomatoes are afflicted with a sort of dry rot – some are healthy and they are a precious delicacy. Maybe August will cool down and Roy and Wayne will be happy with the quality of their tomatoes.

Tony has been very busy this summer and we miss his frequent stopping by. He is working long days at the park,

The Years Come and Go

filling in at the DNR for fire-sighting, etc. He's also busy keeping in touch with Jenny who is working in Austin for the summer. She will be done on August 11th and then will spend some time at home until school starts again. They are making plans for their wedding next June.

Morgan celebrated her third birthday last Sunday. She is so vibrant, active and cute! I think her speech is improving some. She knows that Mommy has a baby in her tummy.

Joyce keeps busy teaching summer school and working at Lake Country. Sharon's knee is giving her lots of pain. She is doctoring and if she needs surgery, I hope they do it before she has to start school.

We are waiting patiently for Katie's baby to join us. Bill will be home on furlough when that little person arrives. He'll miss so much of his/her development while he is gone…..I feel bad for him. He'll be home for good sometime next spring. Roz's Mark has already left for Iraq……he'll be a medic so I pray for his safety. Roz is ready for school to begin and has found a job to help her with expenses. Lins is busy raising Jack and working. She is thinking of taking the fall semester off because of the stress she experienced last spring. Hannah and Jena are both getting ready for their senior year. Jena said that she is ready to move on. Hannah spent a week with CHIC in Tennessee in July.

Roy and I are just living basically. This heat is hard on (old?) people.

August 5

Last night I poured out my heart to the Lord – for my people and for the people of the world. Oh, God, bring each one to a real awareness of you. Help each one, Holy Spirit. Cause each one to yearn for Your presence in their lives; to accept and take hold of Your love for each one. Cause each one to want Jesus Christ as part of their living, to accept Him as their Savior and Redeemer of their precious souls. There is power in the blood of Jesus which He shed on the cross – for sinners who are saved by His grace through His son, Jesus Christ.

November 24

Such a long time since I wrote – where to start?

Little Evelyn Rose arrived on August 19th…..eight pounds and 20 inches long. Such a sweetheart with dark hair and dark eyes. Bill got to come home for her birth but had to leave again after ten days – what a sad time for him and Katie! Roz, Lins, and Jack are with her, but she misses Bill greatly.

We had a very dry fall. The leaves turned brown but when it rained a little, they greened up for a while. The gardens produced abundantly considering how little rain we've had. The tomatoes were excellent; in fact, I still have six tomatoes in the fridge. We had BLTs on Wednesday, and they were still good. The beans didn't produce during the summer as they are supposed to do. But they stayed green and then when it rained, they blossomed and were very good. Odd!! All in all, it turned out to be a good garden.

This fall, Wayne reconstructed his corral – a lot of hard work but he feels that it will last. He also had the Quonset tinned. That too was a lot of hard work, but he and Roy both felt that it was needed.

Linsay, Jack, Roz, Katie, and Eva spent some time on the farm in October – such a joy to have them around! Little Eva is growing and is so cute – she has a beautiful smile when she wants to use it. Katie calls her a "high maintenance baby" but she is such a sweetheart. Nobody from a distance came home for Thanksgiving, but almost everyone will be here for Christmas. Thanksgiving was at Joyce and Rod's; they did a great job of hosting us all. November has been an unseasonably warm month – a few periods of cold but mostly in the high 40s and middle teens at night. We did have a couple of snow days, but the snow always melted.

On November 9th, I had aneurysm procedures on two arteries leading into my legs. The one they tied off completely and the other one, the doctors "packed"……whatever that means. On December 8th, I will have the third one taken care of; this is bigger and they have to do surgery and put in a stent. My legs seemed to go "berserk" after the first procedure. They are getting stronger and I'm hopeful that trend will continue so that I can walk in comfort again.

November 27

It's four o'clock in the morning and I can't sleep, so I decided to get up and write in my journal. The weather is definitely becoming winter. It was about 20 degrees for the high yesterday – now that isn't really cold but it was raining and felt raw. I just checked the thermometer…..15 degrees.

Pastor Bill told us yesterday that he and Yvonne are moving on for the next phases of their lives. He's been our pastor for ten years and I've grown to love and respect them both very much. I'll miss them a lot. (I hate change!) I wonder what God has in store for our little church.

November 29

The forecast was for snow, but guess what – a tiny skiff of snow and rain! So, that makes for icy roads. I believe the sun is going to shine today though and that will be great. It's been so cloudy and overcast. One's attitude surely changes with the weather. (It did get colder....0 degrees this morning.)

December 19

My so-called "musings" have slipped. The fall was nice and long. The crops have all matured and ripened; the farmers got their fields ready for the next season; the gardens just kept yielding – a great fall for tomatoes, peppers, etc.

November and December have been a bit unusual. The skies in November were largely cloudy but the temperatures were above normal – not much moisture, but enough to satisfy us. The temperatures in December have been way above normal. We have some snow on the ground that's nice and white. Every time the temperatures rise close to 30 degrees, I hold my breath that the snow won't melt.

The surgeries for the aneurisms have been completed and I am on the mend. My legs still give me trouble if I attempt to walk for a long time. God is working every minute to heal me and I thank Him for His care. Judy was with us four days after the last surgery, and it was so comforting to have her here.

Wayne got us a Christmas tree from his own tree farm and Judy decorated it; it's so pretty! What would I do without the love and care of my family. I thank God for each one, the men as well as the women.

Christmas is just around the corner. Everyone will be here, except Zach. Jenny and her family arrived yesterday.

2006 Calendar Summary

January's temperatures went below zero only one day.....20 below on the 19th. The rest of the month was mild with temperatures ranging from ten to thirty degrees, accompanied by bright sun, a little wind, some dreariness, and nine inches of snow. Mom used phrases such as "exceptionally mild," "beautiful sun," and "lovely day" to describe the weather. February's weather was more variable.....15 and 20 below at the beginning; 45 below in the middle; and 25 below to 30 above at the end of the month. The cattle's water froze on the 18th. The doctor told Dad his prostate was very good for his age.

Eight little calves were born in March. The first two weeks of the month were mild, followed by a cold spell, and ended with temperatures in the 30s, 40s, and 50s. Joyce stayed overnight on the 9th and Judy arrived for a week's visit on the 15th, which Mom characterized as sunny and nice weather, but not springy. Seven calves, including twins, were born in April, but, unfortunately, one little guy died. The weather was

The Years Come and Go

beautiful with temperatures in the 50s and 60s, reaching a 75-degree high on April 17th. Palm Sunday, Good Friday and Easter Sunday were lovely days. On April 24th, it was very cold with a north wind and a high of 50 degrees.

One little calf was born on the 29th of May, and the bull jumped the fence while the cows were residing in the east pasture. It froze hard on the 20th of May.....the following week temperatures soared to a high of 75 degrees, then 88 and 90 degrees on the 28th. The remaining days of May alternated between "absolutely gorgeous" with temperatures in the 70s and "so cold" with highs in the 50s and north wind.

Dad and Wayne went fishing on a lovely day the first week of June. Temperatures in the 70s persisted throughout the month, except for a few days when the thermometer registered in the 80s. On the 26th, terrible storms hit areas around the farm. Wayne baled hay on the beautiful last three days of the month and finished baling on July 2nd. A cow received a shot on July 3rd. According to the data on Mom's calendar, July was a hot month with temperatures registering in the high 80s and 90s. Katie, Linsay, Roz and Jack came home on the 15th.

Invigorating! That was Mom's word to describe the first week of August which also featured a gorgeous rainbow. A tornado hit Warroad on the 5th, and an inch of much-needed rain blessed the farm on the 13th. Temperatures settled in the 70s for most of the month. Evelyn Rose was born on the 19th. Jon and Judy spent time on the farm and went with the family to Duluth on the 20th. The cows were in the southeast and east pastures.

September began with a "cooling off period" that threatened frost at night. In the middle of the month, people were treated to an Indian Summer when the temperatures settled in the 80s. Beautiful foliage and fall weather (50 degrees) – but no frost – ended the month. Jenny, Andrew, Katie and Eva were home for a visit and for Katie's shower on the 10th. September produced one little calf.

Spectacular foliage and beautiful weather characterized the first week of October…..but there was an infestation of ladybugs (I wonder if they were actually the vicious Japanese beetles that look like the gentle ladybugs). Then it turned abnormally cold for the month (25 degrees) and temperatures continued to drop, except for a nice fall interlude in the middle of the month. Two to three inches of snow fell on the 31st. The cattle were tested on the 10th and everything turned out okay.

Both November and December were mild months with temperatures above normal. On November 5th, Mom wrote "Spring has sprung……sunny and 50 degrees." On December

1st, it was 10 degrees and snowing beautifully. On the 3rd, it was 15 below and the water froze. On the 7th, it was 20 below and Mom and Dad went to Grand Forks. For the rest of the month, above normal temperatures continued with little snow.

Chapter 11

2007, 2008

(2007 journal entry and calendar summary and
2008 journal entry and calendar summary)

Hope that is seen is not hope. For who hopes for what he sees? But if we hope for what we do not see, we wait for it with patience. Likewise, the Spirit helps us in our weakness. For we do not know what to pray for as we ought, but the Spirit himself intercedes for us with groanings too deep for words.
Romans 8: 24-26

2007 Journal Entry

April 27

It's been a long time since I wrote anything. The winter passed. It was a very cold winter in February and somewhat cold in March – not too much snow though. By the end, we were yearning for spring to come and it did. Now I'm waiting patiently for all things to start growing (always waiting for something!).

I've been feeling pretty good – some days better than others. Stamina is down but, with God's help, I'll do what I can. Each day, every hour, I praise God for His presence and faithfulness. He has given us so many gifts. By His grace, through Jesus Christ, He has saved us unto eternal life. I have so many precious children, grandchildren, and great grandchildren – oh God, how I thank you for each one!

Judy was here in March. She'll be here again for Tony and Jenny's wedding on June 30th. Katie, Linsay and Roz are so good about coming home as often as they can. Pam and Wayne have their whole family with them this weekend. It's Hannah's last high school prom – doesn't seem possible.

2007 Calendar Summary

The annual Clasen Christmas party on January 1st heralded the mild weather in the first week of the month. On January 10th, it snowed two inches and then the temperatures dropped to below zero (15-30 degrees) for a few days. Mild temperatures (20 degrees in the daytime to around zero at night) marked the rest of the month but weren't sustained during the first two weeks of February, which hosted temperatures in the 15 to 35 below zero range. On February 16th, Mom wrote "Above zero!" It was 20 degrees above zero and climbing with a little snow falling to whiten things up a bit. A little calf was born on February 26th, and Wayne went to the Cities on the 27th.

March brought more mild temperatures – in the 20s and 30s – and mostly beautiful weather with an occasional nasty day. Most of the snow melted on March 11th. Five little darlings were born during the month, but two died……Mom was so sad. Judy came home for a week. Mom had a hair appointment on March 13th.

Full winter returned on the 2nd of April with rain, snow and a cold north wind. It didn't last long, however, and lovely spring days followed and continued for most of the month. Temperatures ranged from highs of 43 to 70 degrees. Mom and Dad planted onions and peas on April 28th.

Warm days and cool nights were the hallmark of May with southeast winds, quite a lot of rain, and temperatures ranging from 55 to 88 degrees. The cows lingered in the east and then in the southwest pastures. One little calf was born at the beginning of the month and five more followed in June. All was well. Myrtle's funeral was held on June 1st, Jen's shower on the 10th, and Tony's wedding on the 30th. Temperatures soared in the middle of the month (90 degrees) and then cooled down by the end. The cattle were moved from the east pasture to the south pasture. Pam and Wayne went to Duluth, and Wayne cut hay when he returned.

Mom and Dad went to Fargo in July on a day when it was 80 degrees and very humid. The weather vacillated between mostly gorgeous days (70s and 80s) and a few unbearably hot ones (94 degrees). Mom and Dad picked blueberries on the comfortable days. A little calf was born on the 25th, and the cows remained in the southeast pasture. Mom had her hair done on July 13th.

August was a cooler and more comfortable month with temperatures averaging 50-60 degrees. The cows traveled: west, southeast, east, and southwest. Thirty-three dollars were spent on chicken feed. September began on a hot note – 91 degrees – and immediately cooled down so that it froze on the 11th and again on the 14th; this time it was a hard frost (26 degrees). On September 20th, it was a beautiful, sunny fall day. It was very windy with a high of 90 degrees on the 23rd.

Wayne began feeding the cows on October 6th. Mom made a trip to her hairdresser on October 16th. October was an interesting weather month: 70 degrees and sunny; three inches of rain; temperatures in the 40s and 50s; and snow flurries on the 31st. Temperatures were above normal for November. There was no snow for opening hunting weekend which hosted ten hunters, including Judy and Bill. Temperatures went back and forth from a 30-degree to a 45-degree high. Mom and Dad went to Tucson for Thanksgiving on the 22nd and Willie and Jenny's wedding on the 23rd ("beautiful!"). After enjoying spectacular weather in Tucson, they returned to a week of cold weather (15 below) and snow on the ground.

It snowed four inches on December 1st, two more inches on the 2nd, and three more inches on the 6th. It was cold for the first few days of the month (20 below), and then temperatures warmed to highs in the 20s. They stayed there for the rest of the month, including Christmas when it was 20 degrees and very white.

2008 Journal Entry

October 1

A lot of water has passed under the bridge since I last wrote which was a year and a half ago! Time flies by so fast. It seems like yesterday that Eva was born; now she is a lovable little two-year old and the apple of her Papa Wayne's and Grandma Pam's eyes. Thank you, God, for her – bless her and keep her close to You as she continues to grow.

Tony and Jenny are living in the Fargo-Moorhead area. Jenny's job is going well. Tony is working for Schwann and likes the job but says it's for bachelors – he never gets to see

Jenny so he's looking for another job. What does God have in store for them? I pray that they will seek Him and give Him all their ambitions and problems so that He can guide them all the way.

Will and Jenny are very happy doing what they love in San Francisco…..don't get to see them much but we keep in touch. My prayers for them are constant – praying that they too are seeking Christ and have accepted His greatest gift: eternal life through His precious blood.

Little Autumn came into this world and is a blessing to us all. She's so cute and very much her own person. Take care of her, Lord – guide her, keep her, and mold her as she continues to grow.

How we thank You, Lord, for little Megan. She is such a joy to Jenny and Jesse and all the rest of us…..cute and cuddly and easy-going (I think). Big brother Andrew now has someone to fuss with. God, thank you for these little precious gifts from You. Lead them to love You, to trust You and live for You.

Hannah and Jena both graduated from high school and are attending college to prepare them for the future. Hannah is fighting asthma but, hopefully, it will be arrested and under control. Both are very pretty, young ladies but so different.

They keep us guessing as to which way they are going. They need you, Lord, every hour of every day. Keep them both in Your care.

Zach is still working as a reporter in New Jersey or New York. Jon graduated from the University of Wisconsin and then proceeded to spend nine months in Bolivia and other parts of South America.

2008 Calendar Summary

> (A saying at the top of the calendar reads: Here's to the bright New Year and a fond farewell to the old; here's to the things that are yet to come and to the memories that we hold.)

A little calf was born on January 7th when it was 35 degrees and sunny! Temperatures were unusually high the first three weeks of the month. On the 19th, it was 28 degrees below zero and the thermometer stayed below zero for the rest of the month. The sun shone most of the days, and a bitter cold wind made the last weekend extremely cold. It snowed a few inches.

February started on a relatively mild note (26 above to eight below,) and then on the 9th a blizzard hit, producing two inches of snow and hard winds. The temperature dropped to

27 below and stayed there for the next two weeks. On the 14th, the ski crew headed for Boyne to return on the 19th. February 23rd was a beautiful day, and the men took advantage of the warmth (32 degrees) by going fishing. The rest of the month was lovely with temperatures hovering around 15 degrees. Mom was very sick for several days. Wayne returned home (from somewhere) on the 28th, and Gayle, Bill and family went to Minneapolis.

The first couple days of March were lovely with temperatures in the high 20s, but then it turned cold for a week (25 degrees below zero). On March 11th, Mom asked, "Has Spring sprung?" It was 49 degrees! Temperatures stayed in the 30s mostly for the rest of the month. Six calves were born during the month…..all healthy. Judy was home for a week; Hannah returned from Florida; and all of Wayne and Pam's family were home (they made a snow house). It was a balmy 43 degrees on Dad's birthday. March 31st marked the "last day for winter to roar!"

April was a busy month! Dad and Wayne cut firewood at Ed's the first week when it was sunny and mild (30s, 40s and 50s). Gayle had a party on the 6th when it "snowed all around"……….26 inches fell in Park Rapids. Then it turned warm enough so the tulips under the banking showed their faces, and Mom planted flower seeds. Robins, crows, cranes, geese and a beautiful red-headed woodpecker showed up. The balmy weather held for the remainder of the month, even when another blizzard produced eight to ten inches of snow on the 26th and caused church to be cancelled. Three little calves were born. On April 17th, Mom was praising God for healing Wayne's hand. Nadia was born on April 20th. The temperature soared to 61 degrees on April 30th, and the snow was melting at a fast rate.

The lovely month of May began with a cold north wind and a snow squall which produced huge flakes that quickly melted. Temperatures settled in the 50s the second week and then crept up to the 60s and 70s where they stayed for the rest of the month. Dad left for the hospital on the 12th and came home on the 14th; he had a follow up appointment on the 23rd which went well. Wayne and Pam left for Duluth and Iowa for six days. The cows were tested on May 7th, and four calves were born during the month. On an especially lovely day when the temperature was 78 degrees, the family had a picnic at Hayes. Mom fertilized all her plants.

Reverend Winther's first Sunday at Bethel was June 1st. The last calf was born on June 3rd; the bull got out on June 6th; and the cows dined in the west, east, and southeast pastures throughout the month. Mom had a doctor's appointment on June 2nd, an x-ray on the 5th, and an EKG on the 18th.

Dad and Wayne went fishing on the 8th (caught one fish), the day before Wayne went to Minneapolis and Mom and Dad made a trip to Thief River. Linsay and Jack came home for a weekend. Pine Grove held its reunion on the 22nd, and the family gathered for a picnic at Millie's the next Sunday. The weather for June was mostly beautiful: lots of sun and just enough rain to keep everything growing. Temperatures accommodated anyone who wanted to spend time outside…
……60s, 70s, and 80s.

July was another beautiful month with temperatures mostly in the 70s. Wayne baled hay while the sun shone so that when the storms hit and produced two inches of rain on the 11th, he was finished for the month. Judy came home for a couple of weeks. Mom celebrated her birthday on July 13th with "many calls, cards and blessings from God." Wayne and Pam embarked on a trip to Alaska on July 16th and returned on August 3rd, three days before LeRoy's funeral. Wayne finished haying on the 17th when it was 85 degrees and dug the pond on the 29th when it was a beautiful 72 degrees. There was a family picnic on the 24th, the same day that new chickens arrived. It was 90 degrees on August 31st.

Mom's September weather report included the following phrases: 88 degrees and very strong southeast winds on the 1st; chilly and sunny all day; beautiful 70-degree day; lovely afternoon and evening; rained during the night; 75 and lovely sun; balmy but not sunny; and first killing frost on the 30th. Wayne made a crossing on the 12th. Mom had a hair appointment on the 15th. Mom and Dad left for Toledo on September 26th.

Mom and Dad returned from Toledo on October 5th …… a rainy, cloudy fall day with a high of 56 degrees. One inch of rain had fallen overnight. For the remainder of that week and the next, the days were overcast and rainy and the temperatures fell into the 30s and the 40s. Then, the sun came out and the days were lovely……. "magnificent"….. for the rest of the month. The guys cleaned the hunting shack. Nadia was baptized. Mom had her hair done. Judy and her Japanese friend, Mieko Narusawa, visited the farm for a long weekend.

Seven calves and one bull were shipped in November – a month that began on a surprisingly warm note (68 degrees!), Mom was prompted to write "Could this be November?" Her next comment was "Nasty days!" when the temperature dropped to 40 degrees, then 35, and to a low of 25 degrees with a vicious northwest wind. This was the kind of weather the hunters enjoyed for opening deer weekend. There was a skiff of snow on November 11th, and the water froze on the 21st. The last week saw temperatures in the 30s. Jon arrived on the 26th.

The Years Come and Go

A cold snap hit the farm the first week in December with temperatures dipping to 14 below. It stayed cold for the whole month (12, 25, 28 degrees below zero) with snow falling more or less continually to an accumulation of 12 inches. Christmas Day was "a beautiful day."

Chapter 12

Faith Journeys

> O Lord, you alone are my hope. I've trusted you, O Lord, from childhood. Yes, you have been with me from birth, from my mother's womb you have cared for me. No wonder I am always praising you!
> Psalm 71: 5-6

For the most part, I think Mom was comfortable with our discussions about God and salvation, even when I raised questions that made her either pause to consider or dismiss out of hand. So, I was taken aback when she asked me one night if my faith was still strong......or had it waned over the years. I told her that my commitment to Christ has waxed and waned over the years but, throughout, my faith has remained strong; if anything, it was stronger now than it has ever been. After thinking about her question, however, I realized that my faith really hasn't been the same over the years; that it has been on a journey of sorts, a journey that has been marked by some doubt and a lack of commitment to Christ. I asked her about her faith journey, and she said that she didn't think she had one because her faith had been cemented in childhood and has remained pretty much the same over the years, through good times and bad. Almost as soon as she said that, I could tell she was reconsidering her statement. She picked up her Bible and, after searching for a couple of minutes, found a letter (no date) that she had written to God. She handed it to me and said that she was sorry she had "lied" about her faith and this letter told a different story. A part of the letter reads: *Sometimes my trust and faith in you is so weak. Change me – teach me that I can trust you with my loved ones at all times even though I can't see any reaction taking place. My anxieties get the better of me. Help me, Lord, to become more concerned about those who are in need of companionship and help. Make me more outgoing. Teach me, cleanse me, make me whole. You are the only One who can do this. Margaret*

I told Mom the story of Mother Teresa who endured many years of her life feeling alienated from God but remained faithful to Him and continued her work with the "poorest of the poor" in Calcutta because that was what she believed God called her to do. When asked whether she doubted her faith during those times of alienation, Mother Teresa said that, while she couldn't feel Jesus's presence, she knew He was there in the midst of her alienation; He was always with her. When I asked Mom if there had been times in her life when she felt alienated from God, she allowed that there were times when she felt God was far away – sometimes in her darkest hours when she needed him most – but she would just keep worshipping and praising Him until she once more felt incredible joy at being a Christian. I suggested that she probably did have a faith journey and she should write about it. She shook her head and said, "No, I most likely won't write about mine, but you should write about yours and let me read it when you've finished."

A few weeks later, I inadvertently took Mom's advice in that I was asked to write my faith story as an assignment for a small group I was a part of at church. I called Mom to tell her I had a rough draft prepared and I would bring it along at my next visit. She was happy to hear that and said that she might write one of her own.

When we finally got around to sharing our faith stories, the timing wasn't right. I never did see her story......I don't know that she wrote one. I read her parts of mine while she was in the hospital, and her responses led me to believe that, if she didn't have a written version, she had a faith story in her head, comprised of observations, beliefs, and memories. Based upon our hospital conversations, many of which I recorded, I have tried, to the best of my ability, to present a snapshot of Mom's story along with my own. Mom's paraphrased comments are in *italics*.

Growing up, I went regularly to church and Sunday School as did most of the people in my town. Mine was a fundamentalist church with a kind of "thou shalt not" approach. There was hypocrisy in my church, but there was also a lot of love and concern. I memorized Bible verses which sustained me in tough times later in my life.

I didn't always want to go to church on Sunday, but I never argued or rebelled out of respect to my parents. I also felt good at church, as if I knew that what I was doing was right. I wish though that there had been more emphasis on God's mercy and love for everybody and less on the dangers of hell. Because of this fiery rhetoric, I was sometimes afraid to go to sleep at night unless I prayed that God would forgive me for whatever sins I had committed that day and take me to Heaven if I should die. I worried that God would come for me when I was doing something that He wouldn't approve of, such as dancing or flirting at parties.........and I wouldn't be prepared to meet Him. I must say, though, that I was a "good Christian" in high school and did very few things that I felt would have negative spiritual consequences.

Some of what you're saying, Judy, was true for me also. I loved and respected my parents so much that I wouldn't have deliberately disappointed them for the world. When Daddy decided that he wasn't going to go to church any more, Mama had to take over completely, and she worked so hard to make sure that we got to church not only on Sundays but for special occasions and program practices. That's one thing I'm glad your Dad and I did together ...... it was important to both of us that you kids went to church. I don't remember having the fears of God's wrath that you had. And I don't remember you ever saying anything about being afraid to die. I suppose I was too busy to pay attention to how you were feeling, and I feel bad about that. Oh, and I didn't have any opportunity in high school to do what you would call "bad things".......there was always too much work to do.

In college, I broke out of this fear mold but not entirely. I went to parties with my boyfriend and best friend and generally had a good time. I went to church infrequently and tried not to think about all the "rules" I was breaking. Through it all, I never considered denying my Christian faith and tried to act out my beliefs without sacrificing too much fun. When I went to church, I did so because I wanted to, and I think those times were good for me spiritually. I remember going to a revival meeting with my parents when they came to visit me. A former gang leader working for a well-respected pastor who took drug addicts off the streets of New York and led them to Christ was the speaker, and he spoke to me that night: I wanted to do what he was doing.

I remember that night. Dennis came with us to the revival meeting but he wouldn't go inside the tent. He waited for us outside until the service was over. I remember that he said he was listening outside and thought Nicky Cruz was a good guy. I think your Dad asked him if he believed what Nicky Cruz said and Dennis said that he had faith in God, but it probably wasn't the same kind of faith that we had. He was a committed Catholic. I prayed for Dennis for many years. By the way, I remember Dennis saying that he was proud of you for sticking up for your faith, so I think you were more of a testimony for Christ than you think you were. He even said that you carried a Bible around with you to classes. (I had to tell Mom that the reason I carried my Bible around was because I was taking a "Bible as Literature" course.)

My commitment to doing good things for Christ, ala Nicky Cruz, didn't last, however, and I continued to live my life as I had done before the revival meeting. I think my philosophy at that time was that Christians couldn't have much fun, so I just hoped (and prayed) that I could delay or prevent anything bad from happening to me until I was older and was ready to live a true Christian life with full commitment to serving God. I wanted to be good, to be authentic, but I would not make the sacrifice that I thought I would have to make.

Did I feel guilty? At times, yes, but sometimes what I felt most anxious about, even more than the guilt, was my fate. There were times also when I felt anxious about the hard theological questions: What is our purpose in life? Why were we created? Who was going to go to Heaven? Why do children have to suffer? I kept asking these questions, and there was no one around who could answer them …….. or just assure me that it was okay to ask them. Various pastors told me that I would have to wait until I got to Heaven where God would answer all my questions. I remember feeling uncomfortable asking the hard questions because I thought that entertaining such questions bordered on doubting God's wisdom, and I was sure that doubting was wrong. I also worried about my faith weakening.

I told you that also. I worried about your faith when you asked questions that I thought couldn't be discussed without losing some of your faith. I think I told you many times not to question God, that to question Him would only make your faith weak. My mother told me the same thing when I asked some of the same questions as a teenager. She would say, "Someday you'll know all of the answers but until you get to Heaven, keep your faith strong." And I said the same thing to you. But you have convinced me that God gave us good minds and He wants us to ask questions and even doubt. I know that we can't grow in our faith if we don't wrestle with questions and doubt. I still have a hard time with that, though……a part of me still believes that we shouldn't question but instead wait until God can answer our questions someday.

My spiritual life changed when I taught in Connecticut for two years in that I started going to church regularly and reading the Bible. I was desperate to be a good Christian, to reach out to people who needed help, especially children. Teaching in a low income inner city school in the late 60s, when racial tensions were high, provided me with many opportunities to act compassionately, and I believe that I was a compassionate teacher.

(Mom chuckled a little here. She said that she still remembers some of the stories I used to tell about my teaching days in Connecticut……..how the boys put my bicycle high up in a tree so that I couldn't get it down and how they threw it into the river another time. She said that even though I had a difficult time with some of my students, I never showed any anger toward them – at least she never heard me express any – and she considered my compassion to be an example of acting on my faith.)

It was my two years in the Peace Corps that forced me back to the "old-time religion" of my growing-up years. I felt so far removed from anything familiar that I held tightly to my faith. I was grateful for the Bible verses I had memorized in Sunday School and recited them whenever I felt lonely, afraid, or threatened which was quite often. Psalm 23 was my prayer. I guess you could say that I returned to my faith roots out of a need to know that someone (God) was in control when there were so many times that I couldn't be.

Well, Judy, the little church you attended for so many years while you were growing up was good for you then. I'm glad to hear that. Martha Craven, Harold and Marie Gustafson, Pastor Kronberg and many others……..they loved all of you kids and felt responsible for your salvation. They were good Christian people.

I remember one time when I was in Manila during the monsoon season; the cobras slithered down from the mountains and occupied the flood water on the streets. My only path to the Peace Corps office was alive with snakes and I couldn't stop praying for my safety. Faith in God's protective hand was the only thing that kept me from hysteria. Another time, I was trekking in the Himalayas after my Peace Corps term ended. I was on my way to Mount Everest Base Camp when I got altitude sickness and was scared that I would die of pulmonary edema. When the medical student I was with placed a bag over my head to help me recover, I knew that I was in God's hands. On my way back to Kathmandu, I had two more close calls, and both those times I know that God intervened to save me.

(Here Mom interrupted and reminded me that she sent a letter to the Peace Corps office in Kathmandu, telling me that she

had prayed for me all night long during the time I was in danger. I told her I remembered that letter and the power of prayer it represented. I asked her how she knew I was in trouble and how she could sustain prayer for such a long period of time........and how she knew what to pray for. She said the Holy Spirit led her to pray for me and, while she didn't know the exact nature of my situation, she knew that I was in some kind of danger, so she just prayed from her heart. She said that her faith was so strong, she had no doubt that God would take care of me. She felt close to God that night. Praying made her feel calm when her inclination was to panic. As an aside, Mom said she loved to pray, that praying was something she could do that gave meaning to her life when there was really no way she could serve as a missionary or a social worker who helped people.)

For a while after the Peace Corps, I was diligent in my faith walk. For as long as my memories of my great need for God while serving in the Peace Corps were still clear, I strived to please Him in ways big and small. I worshipped faithfully, taught Sunday School, read my Bible and sought opportunities to put my faith into action. It was a very good time for my spiritual growth.

I didn't do much to grow my faith during four years of graduate work; one might say that I suffered spiritual ennui. I had met Bill, who would later become my husband, in

Thailand and was waiting for him to get out of the Peace Corps. When he returned and we were in school together, I guess we thought we were too busy to find much time for spiritual endeavors.

My attention to God became undivided the day my oldest son was born. I was so grateful to God for my son that I promised Him I would raise this child and any others to love and obey Him. And I kept that promise. For the next 25 years, I was consumed by my determination to give my children a strong faith, something I felt they needed. I was particularly zealous in light of the fact that my sons would be growing up with only one parent who was a Christian and another who was a wonderful father but could not encourage their faith. Bill never opposed my commitment to taking our sons to church and making sure they had a religious foundation, however, and for that I'll always be grateful.

I think you've done a good job of raising your children to love God, Judy, and Bill has been a good father. Now, you should put your faith to work and trust God to take care of them. Bill also. Remember God's promise that He will never leave them. I pray for Bill every night.

There were times when my sons asked tough questions about God while growing up (some of the same ones I was still wrestling with), but they rarely balked at going to church.

I like to think the reason they didn't is because they found church interesting and the place they wanted to be on Sunday morning. It may be the case, however, that they didn't want to disappoint me, just as I hadn't wanted to disappoint my parents when I was young......and as Mom had felt about letting her parents down. Or, they may have just bowed to the inevitable. I smile now when I remember how hard I worked to ensure that my sons were receiving the gospel truth, even to the point of becoming Sunday School superintendent and teaching each one so that I could control the curriculum. I also quizzed them on the way home from church.....not an unpleasant experience, as I remember, but it occurred to me that my motive for listening to the message was not so much to nurture my own spirituality and faith but to cement theirs. Consequently, the thing that grew the most during those years was my reputation as a very caring, knowledgeable Christian mother, and any growth in my faith during that period was unintentional. That changed when my sons left home and I became involved in our small group ministry at church. I availed myself of every opportunity to practice my faith, and it grew by leaps and bounds.

Now my sons have lives of their own. They probably are at various stages of faith, but I don't worry about them. When Mom asked one of my sons about his relationship with God, he said, "God and I are good, Grandma." I think that's probably the case with my other two sons also. I'm fine with that. God will always be with them.

(Mom said, "That's good, Judy." She thanked me for reading my faith story to her.)

Chapter 13
2009, 2010

(2009 and 2010 calendar summaries)

Yours, O Lord, is the greatness and the power and the glory and the victory and the majesty, for all that is in the heavens and in the earth is yours.
I Chronicles 29:11

2009 Calendar Summary

January events included fishing on the 17th; trips to Thief River and Grand Forks; and Uncle Raymond's funeral on the 26th. Mom also wrote and circled the word "Bed" on the 23rd. The first two weeks of January were very cold (minus 22 to minus 40). Mom washed clothes on one of those cold days. Temperatures moderated for the rest of the month (minus five to 20 above)......sunny, crisp days and a little snow. January 31st was a beautiful "spring day."

Judy spent the first week of February on the farm. The weather was gorgeous......in the 30s with sunshine. On February 9th and 10th, it rained and there was water everywhere. Then on the 12th, the day that everyone left for Boyne, it was 20 degrees and it started snowing. By the 24th, it had snowed eight inches. The sun shone often until the 28th when it was blustery and 30 below zero. The last day of the month was sunny and five below.

March came in like a lion at 30 degrees below zero, and then quickly warmed up to 32 degrees until the 6th when it slowly became colder all day long with a strong north wind. The weather was quite steady with temperatures hovering around 25 to 35 degrees. There was a lot of snow toward the end of the month. March 25th was a "Christmas card day" with fresh snow covering trees with a shimmering blanket. Six calves were born, but two of the little darlings died. Eight calves followed in April. Jenny and her family were on the farm the first week. Mom had a stress test on the 8th. Forty degrees and lots of sunshine dominated the first couple weeks of the month. Cloudy days and a cold north wind followed, leading to snow on the 19th. A temperature of 70 degrees produced a full-fledged spring day on the 23rd. A lot of rain mixed with one inch of snow caused the cellar to flood........it was half full.

The Years Come and Go

Here are Mom's weather notes for the month of May (provided to give the reader a sense of her detailed accounts most months).

- **First week:** cold and rainy; 53 and sunny, but chilly; 30-55 and nice day; 30-65, gorgeous; 60, iffy but mostly sunny; 70, evening thunder showers; 40-70, three quarters inch rain, overcast, north wind and cold; 45, overcast and chilly; 32, snow????

- **Second week:** 70, two gorgeous days!!!!; 40-55, rained a little and cloudy all day; 50-55, rained three tenths of an inch and north wind; 25-41, evening sunshine; two tenths rain, nice forenoon and dreary afternoon; 20s, froze hard, sun!!!;

- **Third week:** 32-65, gorgeous drying day; 40-57, beautiful day; 32-58, overcast and a little rain during the day but sun in the late afternoon; 62, spit a little, 57 high, thunder and showers all day; 30-60, nice day; a calf was born overnight; hair appointment on the 25th.

- **Fourth week:** 73, superb day; 52, two and one-half inches of rain, cold and nasty; 40-55, cloudy most of the day; 40, very nice!!; cold and wet – rainy.

At the top of June's calendar is this statement: "The coldest, wettest, freezingest spring!!!!" Judy went back to Toledo on June 1st (a cold, damp, wet, rainy day – 56 degrees for the high), and Pam and Wayne left for a week on the 2nd, destination unknown. It turned colder, so that it froze hard on the 6th. The leaves finally came out on June 9th, and this event heralded warm temperatures in the 60s and 70s. The first day of summer topped out at 83 degrees. Nice thunder showers and slow rains marked the end of the month. The bull got out on June 15th.

The guys went fishing on July 2nd and 3rd and caught their limits. The weather was a perfect 75 degrees. A little calf was born on the 5th. Wayne seeded Judy's land on the 6th and began haying on the 9th; he finished on the 24th. Jenny spent a week on the farm at the beginning of the month. It hailed in Warroad on July 7th. Temperatures were mostly in the 70s and low 80s for the month……..gorgeous days with just the right amount of sunshine and rain. There was a week in the middle of the month and a couple of days at the end of the month where the weather was cloudy and chilly (55-68 degrees).

August brought everyone home for a family reunion on the farm and at Cass Lake. They arrived the week of the 16th and, except for Katie, left on the 23rd. With temperatures in the 70s and low 80s (90 degrees on the 12th) and no mosquitoes, August was the perfect Minnesota month as was September, which Mom described as "a beautiful fall with summer weather." Temperatures continued in the 70s and low 80s until the last week when they dropped into the 60s; the 27th earned the label "nasty fall day." Mom had her hair done on September 4th. Linsay and Isaac were married on September 18th.

Mom wrote about the October weather in more general terms instead of her usual specificity. The week of October 5th was described as a "very chilly week: overcast and windy but no frost." That changed on October 9th when it froze hard and introduced "another cold, chilly, windy week." On October 27th, there was a gorgeous sunrise "that made the whole area look rosy," and it was a nice day. Temperatures the last week hovered around 40 degrees with a little skift of snow on the 30th.

November began on a chilly, overcast note (28-40 degrees) but quickly switched to two weeks of "abnormally beautiful weather with gorgeous sunshine and temperatures" (mostly 40s and 50s). It cooled down into the 20s and 30s the last week of the month, but the days were still "pretty." Thanksgiving was a "little chillier but nice," and it snowed a skiff on the 29th.

It snowed four inches of beautiful snow on December 1st when it was 27 degrees. For a few days, the temperatures were relatively mild (20 degrees to 0 degrees). "Blazing sunshine" and 15 degrees marked December 6th and then it turned cold with temperatures below zero (minus 15 to 28). It warmed up the third week to above zero, and was even warmer the fourth week ...... "too mild for December," Mom wrote. It snowed a lot on Christmas Eve and the blizzard continued into Christmas Day..........accumulation was a foot. Wayne and Pam went to the Cities for the weekend after Christmas. Temperatures fell into the 10 below zero range the last week. Dad and Wayne put the fish house on the ice on December 31st.

2010 Calendar Summary

Twenty-five below on New Year's Day and 40 below the day after, followed by a January warm-up with sunny days and temperatures in the high 20s and 30s that lasted for two weeks. Mom washed clothes on January 21st when it snowed; on the 23rd it was a high of 32 degrees and a mixture of sleet, snow, and rain. Linsay and her family came home for the weekend. The last week of the month was cold with temperatures below zero. Mom and Dad picked Judy up in Thief River for a visit.

On February 2nd, Roy, Wayne and Judy went fishing. Wayne caught a trophy fish – 29 and one-half inches long – which Judy made him throw away, much to Wayne's utter dismay. He caught a huge northern on the 20th. February temperatures were equally divided between the below zero range (five to 25 below) and the above zero range (0 to 25 above). There were several beautiful sunny days and a few cold, windy ones. It snowed five to six inches on February 7th when it was 18 degrees and Wayne and Pam returned from Fargo. They went to Duluth a few days later to pick up skiers and then headed to Boyne for the long weekend. Jean and Norbert visited Mom and Dad on the 26th.

March came in like a lamb and, for the most part, maintained that identity for the entire month. Temperatures held steady in the 40s except for a few days when they dropped to the 20s and 30s and one day when it got down to zero. The snow melted on March 7th. Nine calves were born. During the week of March 8th, there was thick, heavy fog every day. On March 30th, it was 70 degrees.

Easter on April 4th was a "blessed day, all day long," Mom wrote. Temperatures were in the 30s and 50s that week followed by a couple of weeks of very nice days: cool and dry with a fair amount of wind and temperatures as high as 72 degrees on the 14th and 78 on the 23rd. Eleven calves were born on those lovely days.

Temperatures dropped into the 40s and 50s the first part of May with days that were very chilly, overcast and windy and then jumped to the 70s and 80s the last two weeks when the days were sunny and lovely. On May 24th, tornados surrounded the area and a vicious thunderstorm hit the farm.

June temperatures generally ranged from 55 degrees to 75 degrees with storms and tornados threatening on the 17th, 18th and 21st. Around two and a half inches of rain fell during the month. The cows were tested on the 9th, and the bull broke out on the 11th. Mom labeled June a "good weather month." That label held for the month of July (70s and low 80s) until the last week when it was hot, humid and stormy with temperatures hitting the low 90s. Mom and Dad picked strawberries and Wayne hayed during the perfect weather of the second week. Judy and Bill were at the farm for almost two weeks......Katie, Eva and Sam and Jenny, Andrew and Megan were there for a week. Judy called to say that Quinn Peyton Patberg was born on July 23rd, and she and Bill would be leaving for Phoenix to welcome her.

August was a schizophrenic weather month! The first week was marked by days in the 70s and 80s with cool evenings that were perfect for sleeping. Temperatures rose twenty plus degrees to hover in the 90s during the second week, with a weather index of 100 one day. Thunderstorms and tornados surrounded the area, one touching down in Grand Forks on the 10th. The third week was very pleasant with an average temperature in the mid-70s. The raccoons took advantage of the lovely weather and consumed the entire crop of corn. Joyce and family left for Boyne on August 21st, the same day that Gayle had Mom and Dad over for fish and shrimp. Tony and Courtney and Tony's friend, Jason, were home for the weekend. The rest of the month was "downright cold" (50s and 60s with a north wind). Wayne and Pam left for the Cities.

An old-fashioned thunderstorm heralded in the month of September. It rained a total of two inches the first week and another two inches the second week. Mom summarized the first three weeks: "Definitely fall has arrived. The nights and mornings are cool, and the days have highs mostly in the 50s." The campers had a mixed weather Labor Day weekend. Jon enjoyed a ten-day sojourn on the farm, and left on August 22nd, right before three inches of rain fell. The last four days of the month were "absolutely perfect."

The first killing frost took place on October 1st, followed by Indian Summer weather with cool nights and gorgeous days (lows in the 40s and 50s; highs in the 60s and 70s). Katie, Bill, Hannah, Eva, and Sam were home for the first weekend. Judy and Bill went to Phoenix for a few days, and Jon left for Colombia after saying goodbye in Phoenix. The last week of the month was characterized by very cold, wet, and late fall weather with not much sun.

Summer-like weather (50s) dominated the first week in November, but then it turned cold. A foot of snow fell in the Minneapolis area on the 13th; the farm experienced a few flurries. Mom said the basic November weather was low 20s and high 30s…..cloudy and overcast. Her note for November 14th is "Hunting season closed!" (no information on how profitable the two weekends were in terms of the deer count). By the end of the month, 12 inches of snow had fallen. There was a lot of blowing on the 30th and the roads were bad.

Forty-one of the Pearson clan were together for Christmas Eve! Christmas week was mild with four inches of snow setting the mood. Freddie's funeral was held on December 3rd, a frigid day when the cold water froze in the kitchen. Except for the first two weeks of cold weather (30 below), December was a mild month.

Chapter 14

2011, 2012

(2011 journal entries and calendar summary and 2012 journal entries and calendar summary)

The Lord hears His people when they call to
Him for help. He rescues them from all their
troubles. The Lord is close to the brokenhearted;
He rescues those whose spirits are crushed.
Psalm 34: 17-18

Weeping may last through the night,
but joy comes with the morning.
Psalm 30:5

2011 Journal Entries

October 11

Oh, how the years go by! Where do the days and months go? And we just disappear into the past along with them.

The sun is shining today but it is chilly.......fall is here! It rained last night and that excited me because we needed a little drink. My heart is filled with praises to my God who has control over all things. I think I'm going to try to summarize what's happened over the past few years.

- Grandma Rozie died in 2001 at age 97. Norma, Sharon, and Phyllis have all "gone home." Freddie died just a year ago, shortly before Christmas. Raymond and Myrtle have both died. Vivian is 92 and living at the Senior Center in Warroad. Roy and I are both 86 and living at home. Ed died in the 90s and I still miss him. Ocky died a few years before Ed.

- Tony and Jenny were married on June 30, 2007. They were married for about two years and then Jenny wanted a divorce, which was devastating for Tony. Tony and Courtney started dating later on and now they seem to be serious. She is very nice and I hope that everything works out for Tony. It's hard to understand why events work out as they do but I believe that God is in control of us all. I still miss Jenny and I continue to wonder why. Tony lives in Fargo and works for the DNR.

The Years Come and Go

- Katie and Bill were married sometime in 2007. Bill came home from Iraq and they got married before he returned – a very nice, simple ceremony. A very nasty ice storm hit the day we had to go home. What a horrendous ride home......we made it even though it took hours. Chris, Mandy and Morgan slipped into the ditch east of Baudette. They got help and arrived home the next day. Many prayers were sent heavenward and God answered every one. He is so faithful.

- Little Evelyn Rose (Eva) was born while Bill was in Iraq. They lived in Iowa for a while after Bill was discharged and now live in Buffalo, Minnesota. Little Sam joined them a couple of years ago. I think that Sam is going to be Papa Wayne's farming partner someday. He loves anything that has to do with the cows.

- Linsay and Isaac were married a couple of years ago.......they live in Duluth. Isaac is waiting for the Lord to show him where He wants him to serve. He graduated from a divinity college and wants to teach the Bible to those who want to know more about salvation through Jesus Christ. I pray that God will use him mightily. Jack lives with them and he will be ten years old in November – how can that be?! He and

Papa Wayne are best of friends – he loves to be on the farm and has become very interested in hunting.

- Jena is going to college to become a lawyer's assistant. She is studying and working very hard. She has two darling little girls to care for – Nadia who is three and Emmi who is one. I hope that one day Jena will find someone to love and to love her.

- On September 3rd, Rozie and Mark were married at Harbor Falls in Duluth – a very lovely outdoor wedding. Rozie has a good job in advertising and Mark is going to school to be an aeronautical engineer. They live in St. Paul.

- Willie and Jenny got married in November of 2007 in Tucson, Arizona. We all flew to that wedding and what a wonderful time we had. It was a beautiful outdoor wedding. Now they have little Quinn who was a year old this July – another little Sweetie Pie. Oh, but God is good, so merciful and kind. Praise Him, all my family, because He is a great God who loves each and every one of His children.

- Jon is currently working in Colombia, South America, doing what he seems to enjoy doing the most: helping others. He left a year ago and will be gone for another six months; when he returns, he will start medical school. He flew home to be at Roz and Mark's wedding. I think he was one of Rozie's bridesmaids. It was so good to see him.

- Zach is working as a newspaper reporter in New Jersey and is dating a lovely girl, Chelsea, who is also a journalist. He also came home for Roz and Mark's wedding. (Aren't Roy and I blessed? God has given us so many precious people to love and be loved by!)

- Sharon and Shawn and Kevin live in Warroad. The girls have worked as paras at the Warroad School for many years – they both do a great job with the children. Kevin is a welder at Heatmore Stoves and it is so good to have him as part of the family.

- Seth is growing up so fast – 13 now and such a lovely young man.

- Jenny married Jesse and they live in Connecticut. What a wonderful mother she is to Andrew (6) and Megan (3) who keep their parents hopping because they are so active – so cute and adorable. I love it when they spend time on the farm in the summer and run over for eggs and lemonade! Jesse works as a stock broker and Jenny is a full-time mother who does a lot of volunteering at the school.

- Chris and Mandy live in Roseau with two adorable little girls – Morgan who is eight and Autumn who is three. Morgan is doing very well in school and Autumn is trying hard to keep up with her.

- Hannah isn't going to school at the present time, but she says she's thinking about going back. Right now she works at a clinic in Grand Forks as a phlebotomist.

- A few years ago, Bill (Pete) had trouble with his heart……what a terrifying time that was, but he seems to be doing okay. He has to "behave" himself. The rest are doing well, each working hard.

- I can't bring Travis up to date. When Shawn and Kevin took him into their home, he was not very old. He grew up to be a very nice young man, and now he's graduating next spring. He is living and going to school in Red Lake, but he keeps in touch with Kevin and Shawn. I pray for him, that God will continue to guide him and keep him in His care.

- Joyce and Rod and Gayle and Bill keep very busy, but they always have time for us. Pam and Wayne are doing well. Pam works at Social Services and Wayne still has a small head of cattle he enjoys working with. They also are so very attentive to Roy and me. We are blessed!

I've tried to bring everyone up to date for these last ten to twelve years. I know there is a lot more to write, but I can't remember it all. Maybe more will come to me later.

October 13

It rained again last night – one half inch. This is after seven-tenths of an inch yesterday. We went to Thief River yesterday and it was a good trip. Dad is concerned about his eye. I told him how much better it was, but he didn't believe me. I came home exhausted from the day. Today I'm going to plant a few tulip bulbs. Rozie is very sad.....she had a fallopian tube pregnancy which was very painful. Wayne and Pam are with her.

October 14

What a nice surprise – Shawn, Sharon, Nadia and Emmi drove out to see us. I see them at church but we never get to visit. Aren't we blessed – so many who reach out to us and respond. God is good.

October 15

Gayle and I drove to Roseau for Kaylie's baby shower and then stopped at the Pizza Place for chicken and mashed potatoes – so very good but I made a pig of myself. When I got home, I didn't feel well at all. Roy spent time with the guys at the shack. It's a pretty nice fall day – high about 45 degrees with a cold north wind. Wayne called – they'll be home about 10:00. Rozie is feeling better but she is so sad.

October 16

Went to church……Pastor Rick gave a challenging message based on the man who was filled with demons and came to Jesus for help. When life becomes hard, wouldn't it be great if we all remembered to ask Jesus for help? He has all the answers. It's Pam's 52nd birthday. We had coffee with her and Wayne and Joyce and Rod. It was a very good afternoon.

October 17

A very cold north wind…..the high was about 40 degrees and the forecast is for a few flakes of snow. I stayed home all day…..made cabbage rolls and froze them. Robert Olson stopped in and gabbed for a couple of hours.

October 18

Cold north wind is still blowing. We went to Warroad for our flu shots, did a little grocery shopping, had dinner with Wayne and came home. I called Rozie for her birthday.

October 23

Mr. Camping prophesized that today would be the end of the world. This is the second time he's done that – the first time was in May. The first time, people were very concerned and the newscasts were full of the coming event. But this time it hardly made the news. I wonder why he is doing this……I surely don't like it. The Bible says that no one knows when the end of the world will occur…..only God knows the time and the place. Jesus will come as a thief in the night. I'm waiting for that!

Pastor Rick preached on the story of Zacchaeus and related it to us. Jesus knows our name when He calls and He invites us to come and fellowship with Him. We should answer His call and He'll make us into new spirits and change our lives forever.

It's a gorgeous fall day. Tony called to check in. I defrosted the deep freeze…..not one of my favorite jobs!

October 30

Autumn celebrated her 4th birthday. She is growing up in many ways except in stature……very petite and lovely. Chris and Many served a delicious supper. Today is also Kevin's birthday.

October 31

It's a gorgeous Halloween night – no snow, rain or anything to hinder the little ghosts and goblins. Emmi, Nadia, Morgan and Autumn were here for trick or treat.

November 5

First day of hunting season and what a glorious day it is – 55 degrees and a little wind. Haven't heard of anyone getting his deer yet but maybe tonight I'll get some news. It's wonderful because so many of my family came home – Judy and Bill, Willie and Quinn, Zach, Katie, Eva and Sam, Linsay, Isaac, Jack, Rozie and Mark, Hannah, Tony and Courtney, Chris, Rod and Joyce, Gayle and Bill, Seth, Nadia, Sharon, Kevin and Shawn, and Wayne and Pam. Now that makes for a real gang…..a great bunch of lovely people! As I visit with each one, I thank God that each is His child. I praise Him for cleansing us from all sin and walking with us down the path that leads to eternal life. Come, Holy Spirit, and guide us to our Heavenly Home.

We went to Warroad and while standing in the Cenex store, waiting for Roy to gas up, I suddenly just toppled over. Everyone was so kind. As it turned out, I cut a gash in my right elbow, my thigh swelled up when I landed, and my lower back turned black and blue and is quite painful. I wonder why this happened..….God knows though, and He'll take care of it.

November 11

All is quiet on the home front. We had a wonderful opening deer weekend. The hunters weren't too successful (three deer), but the weather was lovely.…too nice for November. I think a good time was had by all, even though the deer were scarce. It was fun getting to know 15-month old Quinn a little. She is a lovely little person.……so delightful. God has big plans for her, I'm sure. I pray that Willie and Jenny will teach her about the great love of Jesus. She wore Judy out, I think. God knows best: having children is for the young. Thank you, God, for the delightful people in my life.

November 16

I think the hunters have "hung it up" for the season – still just three deer. This morning the temperature was down to 15 degrees, but the sun is shining so brightly. No earth-shaking news..….just tussling along.

Joyce called yesterday. She has become emotionally involved with a new little girl at school, Gwen, who has a terrible home life. But Joyce sounded more optimistic. I pray that this little person who is carrying so many burdens on her shoulders will know that God loves her and her sisters. I pray for Joyce too, that she will be able to help this family.

It snowed some last evening – not much, but Wayne said the roads were very icy going to work this morning. Roy's cold is a little better. Judy called to tell us that she will be coming home in December.

November 22

Hunting is definitely over......they have five deer and I think that's enough! Winter has set in – a little snow (about five inches) and temperatures getting as low as five below. Thanksgiving is just a few days away. Not everyone will be at Joyce's because they were here for hunting. It's great to have them if they can make it.

Roy's cough doesn't seem to be getting better. Maybe he'll get some medication today. He probably shouldn't have been out this morning when the truck picked up the young stock Wayne had ready for the market. I always hate to see them go.......the mothers really miss their little calves.

Very sad news: Daniel Brandt died; he was only 51 years old. We never know when God will call us, so it's important that we are ready to meet Him at any time.

November 28

Bill has a doctor's appointment in Grand Forks for a checkup so I also made an appointment. It's good when we can go together. Thanksgiving at Joyce and Rod's was wonderful, as usual. I ate too much, but that's not unheard of. It was so good for all of us to be together.

December 28

December is going by so quickly. It continues to be extremely warm with little snow. Everyone enjoys the mild weather, but we do wish for a little more of that pure white stuff. Judy was home for a week early in the month......it was wonderful to have her here, as usual.

On the 15th, I had a pacemaker inserted. I think it must be working because I have more energy.

Our Christmas gathering was a little smaller this year – only 22 precious souls celebrating the birth of Jesus with us. It was not a white Christmas, something we all wish for every year (and usually have it), but the meal was delicious and Pam's tables were so pretty.

I can't remember if I wrote about hunting – what a gang! Bill, Judy, Zach, Willie, Jenny and little Quinn were all here. It was good to get to know Quinn a little......we love her so

much. She kept Judy on her toes! Katie, Eva and Sam came…..
so did Linsay and Jack and Rozie, Mark, and Hannah. Then
there were all of those who live nearby. Oh, what a joy to have
so many of our loved ones with us! They didn't get many deer
this year, but everyone seemed to have a good time together.

2011 Calendar Summary

The first and second weeks of the month sported "perfect January weather: cold, crisp, and sunny, for the most part." Temperatures were at or slightly below zero. They plummeted to 40 below the third week and moderated to 20 below the last week. A total of six inches of snow fell during the month……a few of the days were nasty, but the majority were bright, sunny and cold. Dad had a doctor's appointment on the 21st, and Mom and Dad went to Bible study on the 30th.

February began with a cold snap (35 below) and then it warmed up (30 above) with snow turning to rain. The cold snap returned followed by another warm-up period…..30s in the wake-up time and up to 40 for the high. The last week of February was in full winter mode with temperatures ranging from ten below to five above and a lot of snow and cold wind. Dad had two doctor appointments during the month, and Jack visited for a long weekend at the beginning. Wayne and Pam made their annual ski trek to Boyne.

The Years Come and Go

March came in like a lion and went out like a lamb. It was sunny and cold with temperatures in the 18 to 20 below range to begin with, and sunny, chilly and beautiful with temperatures in the 20s and 30s (one day of 40) at the end of the month. Seven calves were born during the week of Judy's visit. Dad had another appointment with Dr. Ababi.

Five calves were born during the first two weeks of April when the weather vacillated between a nasty, dreary damp day with 35 degrees and a beautiful spring day with 50 degrees. Two to three inches of snow added to the snow piles still dotting the yard. The road to Raygene's became impassable due to the melting snow during sunny days when the temperatures hovered around 50 degrees. It continued to freeze most nights. Mom and Dad went with Pam and Wayne to Katie's the weekend of the 15th. Mom transplanted tomatoes on the 25th when it was 60 degrees. Just when the water was going down in the yard, it rained hard and the yard flooded again. Dad took the banking away on April 29th.

Snow, water, and cold marked the first day of May. On the second day, snow started melting in 60-degree temperatures, and mud was the result. It was 70 degrees on May 8th and then cooled down to 45 degrees at the end of the week. The bull broke out, and four calves were born, including twins, one of which died. Mom and Dad planted seven rows of potatoes and onions the third week of May when temperatures soared to the mid and high 70s. On the 21st it rained all day and night. Temperatures dropped low enough on two nights to freeze.

June: "Some beautiful sunny days but mostly cold, damp and chilly." Wayne finished seeding, etc. on June 11th when the night before it had been very close to freezing. He and Pam went to Minneapolis on the 17th and then on to Buffalo for the weekend. Mom fertilized on the 18th when it was cool and overcast. Jack visited the weekend of the 25th when it was gorgeous. Two inches of rain fell so hard and fast on the 26th that it was perceived to be a deluge. The month ended on a beautiful note of 80 degrees.

In July, Hannah came home; there was a picnic at Shawn's; Mom and "the girls" spent the night in Grand Forks (fun!); and Wayne started haying the first week (75 bales by the end of the week). The gorgeous weather (70s and low 80s....no humidity) allowed him to continue haying the next week. A heat wave hit throughout the country on the fourth week of July.......100 degrees in some places; 90 degrees on the farm with terrific storms of sheet rain, wind, thunder and lightning. The last week was very comfortable and lovely. Katie and her family came for a visit. Dad had his blood tested on July 20th......everything was good.

August began on a heat wave note.......85-90 degrees with hot humid nights. The temperature moderated to a pleasant 70 degrees the second and third weeks – pleasant days and cool nights. Daniel worked on the shed. Wayne and Pam went to Minneapolis on the 19th and to Duluth on the 31st. Jenny and her family plus Jack, Eva, and Sam spent a week on the farm. Except for an 86 - degree day, the last week was lovely with upper 70s, a little rain, and very comfortable sleeping. Hannah turned 22 on August 15th.

Roz and Mark had a beautiful wedding in Duluth on September 3rd. Mom and Dad had a great weekend with everyone who attended the wedding. The weather was gorgeous the week they returned, and then it turned so cold that a hard frost for three nights in a row killed everything, covered or not. The gorgeous fall weather returned the third week and stayed for the remainder of the month. Mom had a hair appointment on September 19th.

"Summer……high temps, no frost, and very windy!" So begins Mom's calendar for October, a month that showcased Minnesota's finest. The weather turned fall-like with temperatures in the 20s at night and up to 50 during the days. Mom and Dad went to Thief River, and Wayne went to Minneapolis. Sadly, Rozie had a tubal pregnancy.

November was another beautiful month; the weather was "too nice" for the second to the last month of the year. Mom washed clothes on November 18th when it was 15 degrees and snowing to the tune of three inches. Daniel Brandt died on November 20th......so sad. He was only 51 years old. During the third week of the month, there was a warming so that on Thanksgiving at Joyce and Rod's, the temperature was 45 degrees. It began snowing again.

December was an exceptionally warm and mild month; it was more like October with temperatures above zero most of the time. Mom had an angiogram done in Grand Forks on December 5th and a heart pacer installed on the 15th. Pam picked up Judy in Thief River on the seventh for a ten-day visit. Mom had her hair done on the 30th. It was virtually a snowless Christmas, and Hannah was the only one home from a distance.

2012 Journal Entries

January 1

Happy New Year! The old year with its trials and tribulations, along with its many joys and great gifts from God, is gone and the new year with its promises of new joys and gifts of love from God has begun. What does God have in store for us in the year to come? We thank Him for all His blessings this past year and know that He is in charge and will bring many blessings to us this year. You alone, God, know what will happen each day. I place all my trials, troubles, decisions, and joys into Your hands and trust and believe that You can handle it all. I pray that precious souls everywhere will search for Your salvation and will find it through the precious blood of Jesus Christ. Watch over my loved ones. Guide and lead each one to the cross of Jesus Christ.

January 2

December was a very mild month – like October and November. Then January came in with a bang – very cold and two inches of snow. But it quickly reversed itself today, and we are once again enjoying exceptionally mild weather. It was fun to see a beautiful white ground for a few days, however.

I had a heart pacer inserted on December 15th – the surgery went well. For a while after, there were times that I wished I had not done it. But now it is healing and maybe I won't be so tired all the time. I know that I won't be falling unexpectedly and that brings a lot of peace of mind.

Our Christmas this year was small – only 22 present. Hannah was the only one who came home. All the rest had Christmas with their other families. Wayne and Pam are going to Buffalo to have their little family gathering at Katie's, probably next week.

Judy was home for a week in December. She just drops in! They spent Christmas in New Jersey with Zach and John and Dee – had a good week. Little Quinn is being baptized on January 9th so they are going to Phoenix then. God, bless little Quinn as her parents bring her to You as You have instructed us to do. I pray that Willie and Jenny will continue to teach her about the love and mercy of Jesus.

January 10

The weather is still unbelievable! Quinn was baptized yesterday. Judy and Bill flew to Phoenix to be a part of the wonderful event. Jesus said, "Let the little ones come to me." This was just the first step.

Gerry moved to North Star apartments this weekend. I surely hope she likes it there. We're going in to see her this afternoon. Yesterday we spent a good day with Joyce and Rod, Wayne and Pam, and Gayle and Bill…..so good to have loved ones nearby.

January 21

Gloomy days but the temperature is warm – 0 degrees. The promise of snow is in the air. Wayne, Tony, Chris, Bill and Vinji went fishing early this morning. It would be nice if they had a tremendous catch.

Yesterday and last night I didn't feel well at all – pain in my chest and, of course, worry crept in. I drank a lot of water in case of dehydration and spent lots of time "in communion" with my Lord. I do feel better today. "Take it to the Lord in prayer" – best advice.

January 23

Last week the weather turned. We had some very cold, wintry days and one night where the temperatures reached 25 degrees below zero. Today the high was 12 degrees so it has warmed up.

We had a unity church service with Pine Grove and St. Phillips Catholic on Sunday evening. I enjoyed that very much.

February 4

It did warm up again and it's been so nice since. Yesterday Bill drove us to Grand Forks for my appointment. The pacer is doing its job. But, of course, I knew that because my energy level is so much greater.

We had three days of fog, and yesterday was very bad. I was thankful that Bill was driving.

Roy, Wayne and Bill went fishing this afternoon. I pray that they get a few keepers. Just after they left, Chris, Morgan and Autumn came and we had a great visit – I hardly ever get to talk to Chris. After they left here, they were headed for Bemis Hill to slide a little if there is enough snow on the hill.

Rod insists that I get my laundry packed up so he can wash it tomorrow. He and Joyce have been doing that pretty much all winter. What a wonderful group of "angels" Roy and I have – truly each one is a gift from God.

This week we heard from Katie. She is teaching autistic children who have a mild affliction full time. Things are going well for Rozie and they are coming home at break time. Tony is busy doing what he has to do and also fishing. Hannah is going back to school in the fall at St. Cloud. Isaac had an interview for a teaching job at the college in Duluth. Linsay and Jack are staying busy. Jena, Nadia and Emmi have the flu with high fevers but they are getting better. Jon has an interview at the University of Washington in Seattle next week and then flies to Montana for something. Seth has a basketball tournament all day today. Andrew lost a tooth during the night and swallowed it – can't you just picture Andrew worrying about how the tooth fairy is going to find that tooth?!

February 12

Today is Joyce's birthday and would have been Freddy's 74th birthday – I do miss him! The weather has been a little more like winter lately – some sub-zero temperatures along with a little snow. We had about two inches a couple of days ago and everything looks so clean and pretty. We had three days of very heavy fog – lots of beautiful hoar frost but dangerous driving conditions.

Vivian died and her funeral was on Monday. Jared Gustafson spoke and Rhonda sang "Serenaded by Angels" – very touching. She was so ready to go home. I'm a little jealous – how happy she is now!

This is Presidents' Day weekend and that means skiing at Boyne. Wayne and Pam left yesterday afternoon and stayed with Isaac, Linsay and Jack last night. I suppose they are well on their way to Boyne by now. Jenny, Megan and Drew arrived at Judy's yesterday so I suppose they too are Boyne-bound. Jenny, Willie and Quinn will be there. Oh, what a great time they'll have together! Joyce, Rod and their family are spending the weekend in Grand Forks, swimming their hearts out. Maybe they'll turn to fish!

Jon got accepted to the medical school at the University of Washington in Seattle and he is existing somewhere between the earth and the sky! What a great testimony that God hears our prayers and answers them according to His will. Now, if Isaac could soon hear about his job to teach the Bible, that would be great!

I'm going to make a pot of soup for those of us who aren't doing anything special.

February 21

What a gorgeous day! It snowed about six inches last night and it's still coming down – the temperature is 28 degrees and there's white everywhere!

March 3

A little trace of snow last night. Tornados are ripping across the country – a horrific one passed through Missouri and the area around it. Today several hit Illinois, Indiana, and Ohio. Dear Lord, comfort those poor people. Oh, that people would ask You, would seek You.

Judy is coming home next Thursday and is planning on staying for two weeks.

April 27

Brrrr – another cloudy, raw day! March and April seemed to have changed places this year. In March, the plants actually began to grow. So many of the days in April have been cold and dreary. Rain is forecast all around us but we remain dry. The flowers and trees are growing and budding but not very fast. It freezes pretty hard every night. April has been a vacillating month – we have a couple days of gorgeous weather and then everything shuts down and it gets really cold. It freezes so hard that I don't dare plant our garden. On the 12th, we did plant some peas and onions.

When Judy was home we went to International Falls to see Joan. It was a nice visit and I think she enjoyed seeing us. We also visited with Helen. Judy gets everyone going around here!

Wayne and Pam are in Duluth. They left here early Thursday morning. Linsay had her leg surgery on Wednesday, so they are helping her out for a couple of days. I talked to Wayne this forenoon and all is going well. Katie, Eva and Roz are coming tonight to spend time together.

Hannah met Jon in Quito, Equador. They are going to explore together, doing lots of exciting things that I would never have dreamed of doing, even when I was young. Jon has finished his job in Colombia and both he and Hannah will be back in the States around May 1st. Then Hannah will come home and Jon will get ready to start medical school in Seattle. I'll be happy to have them both back home. I pray for God's protection for them as they explore.

Judy spent a long weekend in Phoenix with Willie, Jenny

and, of course, Quinny. She had a wonderful time continuing to develop her relationship with "the little one."

Easter was early this year (April 8th) but the weather was beautiful. The snow has been gone for weeks so it was nice and dry for the Easter egg hunt. No one came home from a distance, but we still had 23 people. First, we went to church to praise God for his greatest gift to mankind - his precious son, Jesus Christ. Oh, praise him, praise him! Gayle and Bill served a delicious brunch after church and then everyone came over for the egg hunt.

Bible study is at Gerry's on Sunday. She is going to spend some time with Jim and Amy in Texas because Amy is having a difficult pregnancy. Gerry will be a good person to have around to help the family.

Nadia (4), Rod, and Seth (14) all have birthdays in April. We are having one big party for all next Sunday. Sharon is hoping for nice weather so we can go to the park.

Maybe we'll plant the garden next week. We planted some onions and peas on the 12th and they are slowly growing.

May 11

Writing isn't being done every day, but at least I try to write a little once a month. We had the birthday party for everyone, but it was chilly so we went to Rod and Joyce's house. We had a great time, as usual. The kids – Morgan, Autumn, Nadia and Emmi – played outside and had a lot of fun together.

The garden is planted except for the things that freeze easily. Yesterday the temperature was 81 but today it is only 60 with a brisk north wind, so it could easily freeze tonight. The onions and peas that I planted are growing well. Pam and Wayne gave our yard its first "haircut" for the season and it surely looks fine.

July 1

Must back up a little.........

Spring was early this year. Some very summery weather made us want to do activities that should definitely not be done until the middle of May or later, such as plant flowers and gardens! The weather really cooled down in May. We had a very hard frost that killed tomatoes and other tender plants.

No mosquitos this year.........makes for a perfect summer.

On June 17th, Judy and Jon came and stayed for ten days. A little later, Jesse, Jenny, Megan and Drew came. During their stay, Tony, Chris and Jenny had a surprise 60th birthday party for Gayle. We had all worked hard to keep it a secret from her and we did! She was so surprised!

The party was held at Bemis Hill. There was a total of 34 of us – we had a great time!

When Judy and Jon left the next week, Roy and I went with them for a week. Zach, Willie, Jenny and Quinny joined us in Toledo. Judy and Bill have made so many changes in their home – it's very pretty. We're going to spend the 4th of July with them. Judy called it "Christmas in July." When we leave, Jon will also leave for Spokane to start medical school. Judy is also having a birthday party for Quinny – two years old. She is as cute as a button, so active and good…….has Grandma Judy wrapped around her little finger. She talks like a trooper and is constantly on the go. Grandma Judy will be pooped out shortly.

July 2

Another blistering day in Toledo! We lounged around and went to dinner at the country club.

July 3

I feel so much better. I think it has been the hot temperatures and the trip that took the zip out of me – I have been so tired and pooped out. Quinny is beginning to come around but she doesn't want much to do with Granny and Big Grandpa yet. She is so cute and a little dynamite.

Jenny, Drew and Meggie stopped by Judy's on their way home from the farm. I hated to see them leave this afternoon.

July 5

Homeward bound! We had a great week with Judy's family.....Zach from New Jersey; Jon en route to Seattle for medical school; Willie, Jenny and Quinn there from Phoenix – it was a real houseful! Judy and I went to high tea in honor of Queen Elizabeth's birthday – met Loni and Mary Ann at the tea house. For the first couple of days I was so pooped, due to the flight and the tremendous hot weather – in the 90s. Our celebration of Quinn's birthday featured so much delicious food. Quinny is a little doll who is the apple of Judy's eye – a delightful little person. When we got home we had a birthday party for Sam (3) and Emmi (2). Even though I didn't do a thing, I was tired..... must still be the flight and heat.

We have had such a dry spring and so much hotter than usual. Pam and Wayne visited Katie in Buffalo. They were planting flowers and Pam slipped and broke her ankle in several places. This was a bad time for something like this to happen. Wayne did very well with the housework and yard work, along with the farm chores. I was so proud of him.

July 16

The Roseau County fair began on Sunday with church night, and it will continue just about all week. Katie is driving up on Thursday so they can spend some time at the fair. She is going around by Duluth so Jack can be here too.

August 13

The summer is passing by so fast – soon it will be fall. Of course, fall is one of our most beautiful seasons, but we know what comes next!

Wayne and Pam went to Buffalo this weekend. Little Sam has surgery this morning at 9:15 – God keep him in your care. Maybe now he'll be able to swallow his drool – such a little joy! Pam had her stitches out on Friday so she's on the road to complete recovery.

Next weekend, Joyce and all her family will be driving to Boyne to spend a week with Judy and Bill – what a great time they'll have together! I'm so happy when my loved ones leave to be together, but I surely do miss them.

Mack has been a very sick dog – liver infection and maybe a lot more. Some days he seems better and other days he seems to be worse. I hope he makes a full recovery.

My garden hasn't been the best this year. But LaMay has been so kind in supplying me with what I am craving: cucumbers, tomatoes, corn, zucchini – all is so very good.

We got a card from Kourtney and Kyle announcing a baby in February. She is so excited, calling it the best gift from God imaginable.

I'm eagerly awaiting the arrival of little Isla. I pray that these new parents will teach their little ones all about God and how we need Him all the time, for all our blessings. My prayer list seems to be growing!

Jon has been and is in the thick of things at school. He has a long haul but Jonny will succeed!

2012 Calendar Summary

New Year's Day was cold with two inches of snow and a driving north wind. Winter was short-lived in that the next few days were exceptionally warm, with temperatures in the 40s. A cold snap brought the temperature down to 15 degrees below zero, and it stayed at the below zero mark for a week with another two inches of snow. The guys went fishing on January 21st, a day which marked the beginning of a warm-up with the temperature back above zero where it stayed for the rest of the month. More snow mixed with a little rain caused the roads to be hazardous on the 31st. Mom characterized January as a basically cloudy month.

February began with very heavy fog and mild temperatures in the 30s. It turned cold the second week (minus 12 to 28 degrees) and then a warm-up period produced temperatures in the 30s and a beautiful coating of snow which was appreciated by all. The Super Bowl party at Wayne's on the 5th was a lot of fun. Vivian died on February 9th and her funeral was on the 14th. Wayne and Pam joined the skiing gang at Boyne the weekend of the 17th, while those who didn't make the trek enjoyed a lovely 40-degree day at the farm. It snowed six to seven inches…….. "pretty but treacherous." The month ended at the zero mark with a very cold wind.

Ten little darlings were born during the "lamb-like" month of March which began with temperatures in the 30s, rose to temperatures in the 60s and 70s, and ended with temperatures back in the 30s. Gayle and Bill went to Grand Forks on the 2nd, and Judy came home on the 8th, staying until the 18th. During her visit, she, Mom, and Dad went to visit Helen and Joan in International Falls. Mom had a hair appointment on the 29th. One inch of snow fell on the 30th.

One more little calf joined the herd on the 4th of April, a sunny, warm day (60 degrees) which seemed to be typical of the month. "A glorious day" cropped up several times on

Mom's calendar. She noted that the nights in April were freezing cold, however. She and Dad planted onions and peas on the 12th of the month. Linsay had surgery on her leg on the 25th.

The lovely month of May: temperatures in the 60s and 80s; productive rains; "beautiful mornings and heaven-sent days." Dad planted four tomatoes on May 3rd, and the gang came out to do the annual cleaning on the farm (Mom's Mother's Day gift). Judy supplied the pizza for the event, since she couldn't physically be there. Hannah was back in the United States. Wayne went to Minot on the 8th; there was a party at Malung School on the 17th; and Andrea's funeral was held on the 30th. The cattle were in the southeast pasture where a little calf was born.

The first two weeks of June were very hot, with temperatures in the mid-80s. The last two weeks produced "such lovely weather"……..perfect for Gayle's 60th birthday party at Bemis Hill on the 24th. Judy and Jon came home for that occasion, and Mom and Dad left with them for Toledo on the 27th. The cows traveled from the west pasture to the east pasture where two little calves were born.

Mom and Dad returned home from Toledo on July 5th to more of the stifling hot weather they left behind (high 80s and 90s). Mom's comment for the third week of the month is "hot, hot, hot, hot and humid." Temperatures cooled down for a few beautiful days (high 50s) and then shot back up to the 80s to end the month. Mom had her hair done on July 13th, her birthday. Katie and her kids came home for a visit. The cows resided in the east pasture.

August boasted comfortable weather in the 70s, except for the last week when temperatures soared to the 90s. Two and a half inches of rain fell during the month with a nice thunder shower on the 18th when Hannah and Michael left after a short visit. Joyce and Rod and family went to Boyne on the 17th, and Imo and Byron celebrated their 50th anniversary in Detroit Lakes. The cows utilized two pastures, the southeast and the east, and a little calf was born on the 14th.

Mom wrote two comments for September: "Gorgeous fall weather but no rain" at the beginning of the month and "September was basically very hot and dry (80s) for the last two weeks." The Harvest Festival at Bethel took place on September 9th, Wayne's birthday.

October began on a warm note (80s) with rain which quickly turned to snow when the temperature dropped. Badger and the west area had 15-20 inches of snow! Mom's comment was "What a blessing – very abnormal!" (I don't know how to interpret that comment.) Temperatures hovered around the 40s until the last couple of days when they fell to the 20s and, on one day, eight degrees. Judy and her family visited the farm on October 12th; her family left on the 15th, and Judy stayed until the 28th. One hundred seventy gallons of propane were purchased on October 16th. Zach came to the farm to hunt birds with Chris, Tony, and Wayne.

November temperatures ranged from the lower 20s (one day – ten below) to the 30s and lower 40s. An ice storm on the 10th made for treacherous driving conditions and church was cancelled on Sunday. Thanksgiving Day produced stormy conditions without much snow. Mom had her hair done on the 27th. Judy came home on the 30th. Obama won the election!

A little calf was born on December 2nd when it was 32 degrees and raining…….the snow was almost gone. Wayne sold cattle on the 6th when it was 15 degrees and threatening to snow, which it did: four inches. A little calf was born on that day also. The third week of December was mild with a little snow now and then. The first part of Christmas week was clear and cold (minus 20 degrees on Christmas Day), and the final days featured a warm-up with quite a bit of snow. The Christmas gang engaged in fishing and snocatting on a day that was 18 below zero. Everyone went home on the 28th and 29th.

Chapter 15

The Buzzards of Life and Margaret's Musings

(In 2003, Mom and I edited and published a family memoir called *We Just Shoveled Two Feet of Partly Cloudy*. At the end of the book, there is a piece called "The Buzzards of Life and Margaret's Musings," which Mom wrote as a kind of afterword. I reread this piece and decided that it would be appropriate to include in this book, as it presents, in Mom's own words, a kind of summary of her thoughts about life. For those of you who haven't read *Partly Cloudy*, I think that you will find this piece to be inspiring. For those of you who have read the memoir, perhaps you will delight in her words as if you're seeing them for the very first time.)

I am sure that neither death nor life, nor angels, nor rulers, nor things present nor things to come, nor powers, nor height nor depth, nor anything

The Years Come and Go

else in all creation, will be able to separate us from
the love of God in Christ Jesus our Lord.
Romans 8: 38

I'm reading a book called *The Buzzards of Life* by Stan Toler. The other day I was struck by the author's assertion that God has Samaritans behind every bush or building or battlefront to step up and take our hand when the buzzards start circling. He won't fail us when times are bad. I got to thinking about the Good Samaritan story as it is told in Luke 10: 25-37. At times, it is easier to be concerned about the people of the world than it is to pray for – and be concerned about – our own neighbors. I find this to be true. I see the evident unbelief in someone but dismiss it as "Well, he or she has heard the Gospel so there's nothing I can do." Oh, but there is! A little before Christmas, I gave Leroy an apple pie, and maybe God used that small gesture to help him. Another time, Judy sent me a poinsettia to give to Randa who seemed to be so lonely. Then I learned that she was no longer living at home, but in a nursing home. How very happy she was to see me and receive the beautiful plant! When I stopped by to see her after Christmas, I found out that she had fallen and broken her hip. She loves working with flowers and knitting so, to keep her hands busy, I bought her some yarn, hoping that she would knit some little thing – maybe baby booties.

We don't have to look very far to find someone who is in desperate need because he or she made a bad decision or followed the wrong path, is a different color, or holds a viewpoint that we don't support. We can all be the Good Samaritan and then let God do the follow-up.

Talking about the "buzzards of life" circling overhead – one doesn't live to be 78 years old without having experienced many such times. When Roy was in his early thirties, he battled a case of severe depression that lasted for several years. It was a horrific time for him and his family. I think it was during this period that both of us gave everything to God, for we definitely had no way to survive by ourselves.

Many years ago, I was suffering a great deal with arthritis all over my body. It's painful stuff! It would flair up in one place, do its damage, and then move on to another spot. For the longest time, it settled in my left shoulder. During the day, as long as I was active, it didn't bother me too much. But as soon as I relaxed in bed, the pain would begin. My shoulder throbbed, and the pain was excruciating. Sometimes I'd get up in the middle of the night and lie in the tub filled with very warm water. I tried pills and every kind of rub, but nothing seemed to help. It got so that I hated to go to bed at night. One night the pain was unbearable, and I sat up in bed and cried out to God, "Please, God, take this pain away.

You can leave the arthritis in other parts of my body, but please take this terrible hurt away!" Just like that, the pain disappeared in my left shoulder and it has never hurt again. Since then, I've had a massive heart attack that I survived; I have asthma, high blood pressure, and a lot of arthritis pain in my body, but never again have I had a sore left shoulder. Truly, God answers prayer in His time. I think He lets us suffer sometimes to bring us to the realization that we need Him. Right now, arthritis in my right shoulder and, at times, severe backaches, are keeping me humble. But one day He will take care of them also – in His time and when they have fulfilled their purpose. Jesus Christ suffered so greatly for me, so I guess I can suffer a little for Him. He is unequivocally my Savior, my Redeemer, and my Friend. He loves me in spite of, or because of, my sins. He wants each of us to come to Him with all of our burdens……this is my prayer for all those I love.

In 1995, the greatest life-threatening "buzzard" hovered over us: A severe first heart attack when I heard the nurses say frantically, "We're losing her!" and then another attack a couple of years later. It was then that I decided to have heart by-pass surgery at a Fargo hospital. All the time I was in the hospital, I was never afraid. I had such a calm, peaceful feeling. I just knew that God and His angels were with me at all times – even in my darkest moment when I woke up from the anesthesia and terrible pain wracked my body. Again, the "buzzards" didn't succeed because of all the prayers that were lifted heavenward and because of God's grace. I'm still here and He isn't through with me. God is faithful to all who ask of Him and rely on His mercy. Roy and I celebrated fifty years of marriage five years ago, surrounded by our family, my sisters and brother and their families, and friends. I was not yet "so good" but the gratitude I felt for all that I have was boundless.

The atrocities of living – pain and sorrow – hit us all and God allows them because they draw us nearer to Him and He yearns for our fellowship. We have just two choices when the "buzzards" circle: we can accept His love and healing, or we can reject Him and grow bitter…..and where does that get us? Life at times can bring "a foot of snow" when we were expecting just "partly cloudy."

I think about God all the time. As I go about my daily chores, I pray and reflect on how merciful God is and how desperately I want to be His disciple. What follows are some of my daily thoughts – they are simple thoughts, lacking in sophistication and theology, but perhaps they will comfort and inspire someone along the way.

- A little hurt, neglect, or insult can be the beginning of the end to a relationship. So we need to be careful what we say and be certain that our attitude is right.

- I think of the needs of so many people worldwide and know that I cannot help them all. But if I can help just one, maybe the compassion will multiply and others will be helped too. Make my arms "long," Lord.

- Now that the new year is just about here, I thank you, Lord, for the past with its trials and hopes and joys and thank you also, Lord, for the road that lies ahead. Give me the strength and the faith to follow your path day by day.

- As I think of the past year and thank God for giving me that precious time, I find myself not dreading the future but looking forward to it with wonder………. maybe Jesus will come!

- I recently read a little excerpt about age. According to statistics about age, 78 isn't all that old. But my body tells me that it is. I have a real need for frequent rest. My head feels old when I can't think of the words I want to say to convey an idea or to make a sentence. My memory? Well, how unreliable can it get! I feel old and sad when I think of my loved ones who have left this earth. But it gladdens my heart when I see the younger ones wrestling with the everyday aspects of living. I'm glad I'm alive and able to help them in some way, especially praying for each one.

- Impatience reveals a selfish and often mean spirit, while patience is really an act of kindness. This is so true.

- We receive God's love so that we can reach out and give His love to others. In this way, we receive and give and then receive more of God's blessings. My friend Randa died this past spring just a week after I had visited with her. At that time, I told her that I loved her and Jesus loves her even more. She responded, "I love you, too. Jesus is the one who saves us."

- Each of our days is but a collection of small acts. Each act is accompanied by a prayer that God will knit them all together to make the day one in which His will is somehow accomplished.

- I'm a firm believer in prayer. I pray for just about everything – my children, grandchildren and great grandchildren, my sisters and brother and their families, my friends and neighbors, and even Wayne's cattle that God will keep them free from disease. I pray believing that these prayers are heard and will be answered by God in His time and according to His will.

- We must choose our words wisely. Psalms 141:3 admonishes us to keep a door on our lips. It is better to use our ears to hear – really, what is said – and then we can be slow to make hasty judgments. Sometimes this careful thought will alleviate much anger on our part and on the part of others. It also helps us to become interested in those around us rather than the other way around. If we search for happiness only for ourselves, we miss much joy that can be had by helping others. Looking to Jesus will make us happy.

I enjoy the closeness of family because it keeps me from being lonely. It's a great feeling of security, one that I temporarily lose when everyone goes away for short periods of time. The knowledge of being loved and of loving in return – seeing and enjoying the company of others – gives me excitement, sometimes beyond measure. I believe that family is one of God's greatest gifts and we should never take that gift for granted. I derive so much comfort knowing that my family is praying for me and that I can help them by praying for them. When we're all together, I know that I am blessed.

Chapter 16

2013 – 2015

(2013, 2014 and 2015 calendar summaries)

> Peace I leave with you; my peace I give you. I do not give as the world gives. Do not let your hearts be troubled and do not be afraid.
> John 14:27

2013 Calendar Summary

"A nice January lazy day"……..that's Mom's summary of New Year's Day. The first week of January was relatively warm with temperatures in the 20s, and then a heat wave hit on the 10th with a temperature of 42 degrees! That lasted for a day. The temperature fell to below zero and brought six inches of snow with wind and ice. The next three weeks, Mom labeled "a cold snap." Temperatures ranged from four degrees above zero to 30 below. During this time, it snowed another six inches and the water froze for many days. Mom said on January 27th, "Roy worked very hard on the water." She also mentioned that everyone was home (I'm not sure why people were home.)

The high on February 1st was 32 degrees below zero……. but very sunny and still. It remained that way for the first two weeks…….lots of sunshine and about four inches of snow. Mom had a bad head cold. On February 17th, a blizzard produced eight to ten inches of snow which left everyone blocked in for a couple of days, since the roads didn't get plowed until the 20th when Mom and Dad went to Warroad. Rozie and then Judy arrived on the 19th and the 22nd. The last week of the month featured a very nice warmup, and Mom commented on the beautiful "spring" around the corner.

Mom was in the hospital for a week or ten days the first part of March. Tony and Courtney were married on March 17th, so most of the gang traveled to Temecula, California for the wedding. Gayle and Bill ended up being stuck in Denver on their way home from the wedding. Mom said that, for the most part, March was a very cold month (below zero temperatures and some snow); in fact, it was one of the coldest Marches ever! Six little calves were born during this frigid weather, and one died. It warmed up the last few days in March (35 and 45 degrees above), and those days were beautiful, including Easter Sunday.

Temperatures hovered in the 30s (40 degrees one day) for most of April, becoming more spring-like with temperatures in the 60s at the end of the month. It snowed around seven inches throughout the month……..this accumulation slowly melted, and was replaced by hard rain on the 30th. Bill Starren died on April 9th, and his funeral was held on the 13th. Four calves were born.

According to Mom's summary statement for May weather, it was a cool month which didn't allow for much planting, except for two rows of onions planted on May 7th. Temperatures featured the 30s, 40s (froze hard) 50s, 60s ("Spring is here!"), 70s ("Absolutely wonderful!") and one day in the 80s. Baby Hadley arrived on May 1st, and Pam and Wayne were Motley-bound a few days later. May 18th was the annual farm clean-up day. Judy and Jon arrived on May 21st and Bill on the 24th. They all left together on the 30th. Pam and Wayne and Gayle and Bill both had picnics the weekend of the 25th, a time when the leaves were popping on the trees. Five and a half inches of rain fell toward the end of the month.

The June calendar had this for a headline: "Children will not remember you for the material things you provided but for the feeling that you cherished them"……..Richard Evans. (That pretty much summarizes Mom and her feelings toward her grandchildren, I think.) June began on a cool note.......50s and 60s for the first week which included a couple of nights with mild frost. The next two weeks featured 70s and 80s......very dry with mosquitoes in spades! The guys and Pam went fishing during this time, and Wayne did a lot of planting. Then it was "disastrous weather all around us" but the farm emerged unscathed. On June 25th, it was 90 degrees with a lot of rain...... "a tough day." The last three days of the month ended on a similar note as the beginning – a beautiful, cool 65 to 75 degrees. Wayne and Pam went to Duluth. A little calf made its way into the world.

Hot and humid: July 4th was right in the middle of an 85-degree week with rain. Wayne finished baling on the 8th, and Judy arrived for her 50th class reunion on the 11th and left a few days later when she found out that Bill was in the hospital (she missed her reunion). All of Wayne and Pam's kids and Jenny and her kids were home for the fair – "what a wonderful zoo," Mom wrote. Fair week and the following week were marked by very pleasant, cool temperatures and two to three inches of rain. Mom's note on July 29th reads: "Beautiful, gorgeous days! Temperatures low 70s, a nice breeze with sunshine! We went blueberrying." All the kids went home by the 30th.

August started out with a cool spell (60s) and progressively got warmer...... first the 80s and then the 90s for the last two weeks. Mom said, "The last two weeks have been spent mostly by the air conditioner because of heat and humidity. No casualties though – God is good." A little over two inches of rain fell during the month. Joyce and her family went to Boyne; Wayne and Pam to Duluth; and Gayle and Bill to Fargo. Everyone returned home on the 18th. Labor Day weekend was very pleasant for the "young ones" who went camping.

It was hot (85 degrees) the first week of September; Wayne and Dad started hauling bales. A tornado threatened the Baudette area the second week when it was cool (66 degrees), but nice. Bethel Church had a pig roast on the 15th, the same day that Judy and Bill left for Europe. The rest of that week was cool, overcast and heavy with fog. The last week produced lovely fall weather and still no frost….. wonderful days. Wayne and Pam went to Grand Forks. Mom and Dad went for a long ride with Gayle and Bill……. "It was a good day."

The gorgeous fall weather prevailed during the first half of October with temperatures in the low 70s. Mom and Dad picked green tomatoes to ripen in the house on October 8th. The first snow fell on the 19th, as did the temperatures (30s and 40s). It continued to snow for a couple of days, accompanied by a cold north wind. The sun came out and the snow melted just in time for Halloween. Mom and Dad had the usual four trick-or-treaters.

Winter happened in full force during the month of November. With temperatures settled in the 20s, it was not a particularly pleasant opening hunting weekend, but everyone had a good time. Bill, Judy, Willie and Quinn were the distance hunters. Judy stayed until the 16th. The water froze on November 23rd and then it started snowing. Thanksgiving Day was spent at Joyce and Rod's with everyone having a good time, despite the frigid temperatures.

December was a very, very cold month with lots of snow and wind. The average temperature for the first two weeks was 25 degrees below. For three days, it warmed up to eight below and then temperatures plummeted, so that it was 25 below on Christmas Day. Mom and Dad missed church two Sundays in December.

2014 Calendar Summary

Mom's note at the top of the January calendar: "December 2013 was one of the coldest Decembers on record.......35 below and very cold winds. Now, January is just continuing the trend." And, indeed, it was. There was no church on January 5th due to the 35 below zero temperature. A little warm-up (25 and ten below) provided some relief for three days and then the temperature vacillated between minus 25 and zero for the middle of the month. The Clasen Christmas was held on January 11th, which was a nice day. The last week was a solid 20 below. Mom's note at the end of the calendar: "January 2014 was an extremely rough month…..much severe cold, very windy, and not much sunshine."

February 7th: "So far, February has just been a continuation of January……lots of cloudiness, very cold and windy." Judy left for home on the 8th. Joyce and her family went to Grand Forks and Wayne and Pam left for Boyne on the 14th. It snowed from the 13th to the 17th, and on the 18th Rod and Bill plowed Mom and Dad out……they got stuck! The remaining days of February were very cold and sunny, which Mom said provided a wonderful psychological effect (the sunshine). On the last day, the thermometer registered 0 degrees with sunshine.

March came in like a lion. The thermometer registered a continuation of below zero temperatures for the first two weeks and then pushed toward the above zero mark. Except for a couple of cold days with very strong winds, temperatures remained in the ten to 25 above range. Little Mason was born on March 5th. Rozie and Isla, Hannah and Michael, and Isaac, Linsay, Jack and Haddie enjoyed beautiful, sunny, and relatively warm days on the farm the week of March 9th……… great snocatting weather! It snowed three inches on March 17th and another three inches on the 21st. Dad's birthday on the 29th was 20 degrees and sunny, but then March went out the way it came in – like a lion, facing a very bad blizzard on the 31st. Dad had doctors' appointments on March 5th, 11th, the 26th (Grand Forks), and the 27th. March 16th was Pastor Rick's last Sunday; there was Bible study at Irene's on the 23rd. Eight calves were born in March.

"April gave us a huge variety of weather......mostly though, it was a cold, chilly month." Roseau got 17 inches of snow on April 1st, and light snow fell on the farm for a couple of days. Temperatures were mostly in the low 30s the first two weeks and hovered in the 20s for a week or so before they settled in the high 30s and 40s the last few days of the month. The days alternated between lovely sunshine and windy overcast. Sundays happened to be gorgeous days, including Easter which also marked the congregation's last gathering at church. Dad had a pre-op appointment on April 7th and eye surgery on the 10th. He had an oncology appointment on the 15th and his second eye surgery on the 24th when the rain turned to three inches of snow. Four calves were born in April. Katie called on the 17th and Jon on the 18th. Joyce and Rod picked up Judy in Grand Forks; she went home on May 3rd.

It snowed scattered snowflakes on May 3rd and again on May 5th when the temperature was in the 30s. The snow melted and it rained for a few days so that by the 12th, water was standing everywhere in the yard. The days alternated between sunny and cloudy and the temperature between 30 and 55……there were more sunny days than overcast ones, however. Nadia had her kindergarten graduation on the 15th, and Kourtney graduated on the 16th. Wayne and Pam went to pick up Jack who stayed through the weekend. Tony and Courtney visited on the 23rd. The annual farm clean-up day took place on Mother's Day when it was 60 degrees. Wayne was doing some landscaping which prompted Mom to comment, "It looks so nice!" A storm threatened but passed over on the 24th when the temperature reached 85 degrees briefly. Joyce and Rod planted the garden on May 25th. Judy, Bill, Joyce and Rod left for Norway on the 30th. Three little darlings were born.

Temperatures the first and second weeks of June stayed in the high 50s to 70, with an abundance of rain and even more mosquitoes. Mom fell and hurt her right shoulder very hard so she wasn't feeling well. There were puddles everywhere on the farm on June 15th and lots of flooding around the country. Temperatures climbed to 85 on the first official day of summer and then returned to the 60s. On June 16th, Mom made two comments: "Everyone home!" and "Baby Jazz isn't doing so well." Judy arrived on June 24th and Bill on June 28th. During Judy's visit, we went to see Cy and family and met Joan and Ordean for coffee in Baudette....... "just a real nice day"! In summary, "June was basically a very wet, cool month.....definitely not a summer month!"

July's calendar is replete with news other than the weather. The biggest occasion – one that brought everyone to the farm – was the family reunion held on July 2nd to the 6th. Specific events included the arrival of Willie and his family in an RV which he parked in Wayne's yard; tacos on Wednesday; golf on Thursday; breakfast at Wayne and Pam's; fireworks on the Fourth, compliments of Tony and Michael; and a scavenger hunt and a fish fry on Saturday. Wayne had sprayed for mosquitoes, which helped considerably, but the rain on Tuesday and Friday counteracted some of the positive effects of the spray. Temperatures were on the cool side at the beginning, but the last two days were hot and muggy. Mom mentioned that she was happy to meet little Mason who is "as cute as can be but unhappy with his situation." Wayne started haying on the 7th of July; baled on the 12th and the 13th; and finished haying on the 17th. Mom celebrated her 89th birthday on the 12th when the temperature was 80 and then plunged to 58 with a little rain. Millie had a family party on the 13th, and the next day Trish, Inez, Millie, Gerry and Tootsie came over for coffee. On July 25th, Pam and Wayne took Jack and Eva camping at Camp Cluster in South Dakota. Morgan's birthday party was held on the 26th. Mom's weather comments ranged from "very hot and humid" to "very cloudy and cool all day." The busy month of July.….

August was, by all weather standards, a perfect month with temperatures mostly in the 60s and 70s. Wayne and Pam returned from camping on August 2nd; Mom snapped beans for Pam on the 4th (77 degrees.…. "a perfect day"); and she had a hair appointment on the 6th. The manure hauler graced the farm on the 12th, and Mom ate her first tomato on the 15th. Gayle and Bill went to Tony's on the 16th and then had a fish fry on the 22nd when Tony was home. Wayne went to Minot for work. Mom had an appointment in Grand Forks on the 26th.

Most of September was cool with temperatures first in the 50s and then in the upper 40s. The first frost scare occurred on September 10th, followed by a hard frost on the next two nights. Judy came home again on the 4th and left on the 19th, two days after she and Roy went to Grand Forks for Roy's appointment. Mom had an appointment in Grand Forks on the 26th. On September 21, Judy, Bill and Zach left for a week in Scotland. "Beautiful fall days.…..83 degrees" the last few days of the month.

Until the 14th, October days were sunny with a very cold wind (temperatures in the 40s). It even snowed in Roseau and Warroad. During this time, Wayne and Pam went to Motley; Wayne went to Minneapolis and Rod returned; and Gayle went to St. Cloud. The weather changed, so that the next several days were gorgeous with temperatures in the 60s. Katie and her family, Linsay and her kids, Michael and Hannah, and Tony were all home during this "superb summer week." The month ended on a cold note (40s and 30s).

November began with temperatures in the 30s and 40s, and then on the 9th, Mom wrote: "I think winter is here! It started with a few snowflakes and then continued with more snow." Temperatures dropped to the 20s and lower until it was 0 on the 17th and seven below on the 20th. "Excessively cold days" probably made Inez and Gerry happy that they were going to Hawaii on the 21st. Temperatures moderated for a couple of days (30 and 37 degrees) and then plummeted to 28 degrees below zero the night of the 27th. Roads were hazardous. Judy and Bill were home for the first hunting weekend. They left for Seattle on the 26th.

The sewer froze sometime during the first week of December when the temperatures were in the low 20s. Dad had an appointment and physical therapy in Roseau. Wayne and Pam went to the Pitt church on the 7th, the same day that the gang decorated Mom and Dad's Christmas tree which came from the Pearson Tree Farm. It snowed five inches on December 8th, a beautiful 19 - degree morning. Temperatures rose to 38 degrees for the rest of the week. Pam and Wayne left for Duluth; and Mom made potato sausage with Gayle and Bill and Joyce and Rod. The third week it was 15 degrees and snowing. The fourth week it was 30 degrees and snowing. Mom asked where the sun was hiding. On Christmas Eve, it was 32 degrees and supper at Pam and Wayne's was "delicious". On Christmas Day, Mom wrote this: "Thank you, Heavenly Father, for your gift of Jesus to me!" Very cold days prevailed the last few days of the month (minus 15 and 20 degrees).

2015 Calendar Summary (Mom's last calendar)

> God has said, "Never will I leave you;
> never will I forsake you."
> Hebrews 13:5

On January 2nd, Mom fell and hurt herself badly so she didn't keep track of very many things. Dad wasn't feeling all that well either, so Judy came and stayed with them for a couple of months.

Judy stayed until the beginning of March. Mom: "Poor Bill, alone all those weeks. But I really appreciated her. She is a good nurse! I thank all my dear family for their care and love." Mom got a walker and was told that if she were good and used it, she wouldn't fall again.

(There weren't any entries on the March 2015 calendar. Instead, Mom made notes for March 2015 on the March 2014 calendar in a different color ink. She might have mislaid her 2015 calendar temporarily.) March came in pretty much like a lamb…..50s in mid-March. There was a lot of wind, some snow, and a little rain. After one final snocatting adventure that included most of the family, the snocats were put away. There were ten calves born in March, 2015.

Easter was early this year – April 5th. The weather was very nice, most of the time. The last week of April was a lovely week – highs in the 50s and 60s……..even a few 70s. Farmers were very busy even though it was early. There hadn't been much rain so it was dry. Mom wrote: "But God will send it when we really need it. Put your trust in the Lord."

It was a lovely spring week in May (74-82 degrees) when Joyce and Rod went to New York to visit Judy and Bill. Mom planted begonia bulbs. The second week was cooler (40s) with north wind and frost on May 8th. There was a lovely, slow drizzle all day. It rained most of the third week until the 16th when Mom said that she and the gang got a lot done in terms of housecleaning and garden planting. Except for a couple of unpleasant days with temperatures in the 40s, the rest of the month consisted of sunny days with temperatures in the 70s and lovely, light breezes. Gayle and

Bill went to the Cities and Mom and Dad planted tomatoes. May ended with a frost on the 29th.

June appeared to be a lovely month with temperatures ranging from the 50s to the 70s and two days in the 80s. Mom's comments supporting that conclusion punctuate her calendar page: "Lovely, lovely day!" "Beautiful summer day!" "Gorgeous day and evening!" There was heavy smoke from forest fires in Manitoba. Judy arrived on June 1st and stayed for the whole month. During her visit, she, Mom and Dad went to see Helen (Judy ate a whole jar of pickles!), Inez, and Joan, Ordean, and Norbert in Baudette. Jon came for a visit, as did Katie and her kids. Wayne and Pam went to Grand Forks to visit Hannah who was preparing to move to Orlando. Joyce and Rod had a family picnic to welcome home Nadia on the 14th.

Mom's comment at the top of the July calendar: "The weather is pleasant. Wayne has the haying done but smoke from Canada doesn't let the sun shine through for curing." It was a rainy first half of July with temperatures in the 70s and 80s. Wayne baled 33 bales on July 10th and 16 bales the next day. Judy and Quinny arrived on July 13th, Mom's 90th birthday, and stayed until the 19th. During that week, the Clasens held a huge family reunion on a beautiful, dry day at the park. Dad had two transfusions on the 17th and 18th.

Hospice made their first visit on the 21st and visited again on the 31st. Morgan's birthday party was held on the 25th. The last week of the month was hot (80s and 90s).

Wayne and Pam went to Linsay's on August 3rd because Isaac was in the hospital. They brought Jack and Haddie back with them two days later, but had to return to Motley on the 7th because Isaac wasn't doing so well. Jack helped Wayne with the haying while he was on the farm. Temperatures were in the 60s the first week and rose to 90 degrees on the 13th…..too hot to do anything except enjoy a picnic at Gayle and Bill's. Zekie died and left Mom feeling very lonesome. Judy came home again. Most of the rest of the month was cool (60s and 70s……some 80-degree days), alternating between rain and sun. Mom said that she enjoyed a beautiful day with many of her family on August 9th. Helen and JoAnn came out to the farm to make pickles on the 22nd. Bill Patberg arrived on the 28th, and all the men went fishing the weekend of the 29th.

Mom described September as the saddest month of the year: Dad died on September 21st. Everyone in the family was home for the memorial service on the 25th. After the service, we all celebrated his life with a pizza party at the shack. Mom was happy to be surrounded by her family. She made only one weather comment: "Typical fall weather;

temperatures mostly in the 70s." On September 29th, there was a very hard killing frost.

October's temperatures for the first part of the month fell into the 35 to 55 degree range......gloomy, chilly days as well as beautiful fall days. Judy left on October 13th, and Katie and Linsay and their kids arrived on the 15th. Temperatures dropped to the 30s and 20s the last two weeks with snow that turned to rain on the 28th. Marjorie Tveit died and her funeral was on the 19th. Jena got engaged on the 20th. The cattle were fed on the 28th and the 31st. Mom made sure that all the clocks were changed.

It was snowing hard when Judy, Quinny, Willie and Bill arrived for opening deer hunting the weekend of November 7th. Temperatures hovered around 30 degrees (40 degrees one day)...... "a wonderful weather weekend for hunting," Mom said. Nothing changed until November 19th when it stopped snowing and temperatures plunged to 20 degrees. They moderated a little at the end of the month, but stayed mostly around 20 degrees. Judy left on the 17th; 14 calves were shipped on the 19th; and Pam and Wayne left for Missouri to see Rozie on the 24th. The last little calf was born on November 8th.

(Mom's handwriting had deteriorated so that her writing on the December calendar was difficult to read in places.) Snow and relatively mild temperatures (32 degrees) made for two beautiful first weeks of the month. The snocats made their yearly debut. The third week was colder with a little wind (0 degrees). Mom watched Dr. Salem with Joyce and Rod on two Sundays. LaMae paid Mom a visit on the 22nd, bringing with her delicious lefse. Mom said about Christmas: "What a lovely time we had being together!"

THE END

Conclusion

> God himself will be with them; he will wipe away every tear from their eyes, and death shall be no more, neither shall there be mourning nor crying nor pain anymore, for the former things have passed away.
> Revelations 21: 3-4

Near the end of her life, Mom had to move from the family farm, where she had lived for 68 years, to a nursing home in our small town. She hated to go but health problems required her to live in a safer environment. Prior to Mom's serious decline, she had been quite able to make appropriate decisions, tend to her personal needs, and fully engage others. Because the nursing home was close to her children's homes, someone would visit Mom every day – she looked forward to our visits so very much. We knew, however, that there would come a time when she would decline to the point where no one here on earth could give her the kind of care she needed. Life came full circle for Mom and for us, as it eventually does for everyone – it's the rhythm, the cycle of life.

And now, it's been a little over a year since Mom died. My heart is still full of grief, and I can't imagine a time when it will be normal. I close my eyes and see my parents on the farm...... Dad walking across the yard from the Quonset to the house, checking the tomatoes on the way; and Mom puttering in the garden and then walking slowly over to the barn to spend a little time with the cows. Other images include Dad bringing home the mail; Mom sitting at the kitchen table looking out the window, waiting for whomever or whatever comes into view; both of them taking a little spin on the golf cart, usually with Zeke catching some wind from the edge of the seat; watching the birds and commenting on the trees and the weather from their respective places on the porch – Dad sitting on the chair and Mom reclining on the chaise lounge; and making sure the "pot" was on every day in time for Wayne's 4:15 coffee arrival. There are other images, of course, but these are the ones that float around in my mind. Their days were, for the most part, uncluttered and simple, with few choices and decisions that had to be made. Except for weekly trips to Warroad, birthday parties, and invitations for family gatherings at Gayle's, Joyce's, and Wayne's, they did not have many opportunities or reasons for leaving the farm.

An activity that Mom and Dad enjoyed most of their lives, and until they could no longer participate, was blueberry picking. In *Letters from the Farm*, the author talks about how rewarding it is to find blueberries on the ridge in the summer. She says the reward is felt first in the surprise discovery of a blue patch among the weeds in the woods where the moss and pines offer a soft bed to rest when tired. And then there is the reward of the instant gratification you feel when you pop a handful of the delicious berries in your mouth...... "It's a sweet taste of God's pure earth"! I think this is one image I will carry with me forever: Mom and Dad bent over a blueberry patch on a sunny afternoon, focusing on the task of filling their pails, with only the wind in the trees and the irritating mosquitos sharing their space.

On some evenings, when we were sitting in the front room at the end of the day, I read from a book, *To Bless the Space Between Us: A Book of Blessings,* by John O'Donohue. Mom liked the poem, "For Old Age." There were times when she and Dad expressed regret over the restrictions that old age imposed upon their physical and mental health. Mom once laughingly said, "Those people who write glowing books about the golden age should be shot!" She had me read the poem several times because she liked the language, but she may also have found the content to be thought-provoking, including the last two lines: "And may you find a wonderful love/In yourself for yourself." I wonder if Mom, who directed so much of her attention to loving others, could relate to the concept of loving herself.

Printed in the United States
By Bookmasters